Contents

Acknowledgments:

I am blessed to intimately know people who love God's Word and live by the power of the Holy Spirit. They have given me courage to even attempt to write this book. I am thankful for their example of how to manifest the Lord in the commonality of everyday life. Their prayer has sustained me in difficult times. I am deeply grateful for them all. The original teaching of this material came from a study of the Gospel of Mark. My students encouraged me to bring my informal presentation into written form. Many, many friends made this work possible.

My special thanks go to Jack Milnes for his faithful encouragement and help at the beginning stages of the early manuscript. Ben and Kathy Doerge deserve much thanks for their editing expertise. I am deeply grateful for their competence, love, and generosity. Thanks go to Dorothy Hatsell for her English edit. For the final proof reading, thanks to eagle-eye Robert Weller, my beloved husband. I deeply appreciate his support, encouragement, and quiet strength. In addition many thanks to the computer crew who helped me enter the computer age. Thanks to Mark Smith, Roger Martin, Marty Delfino, and Jack Milnes. Zena Fessler deserves thanks for organizing and doing my mailing list. The really amazing blessing is that each one cheerfully donated time and skill to this community effort. Thanks!

Friends gave financially to this project making it possible for me to leave the active ministry and concentrate on this new assignment. My deep appreciation go to:
Jim and Marge Deardroff, Marty and Janet Delfino, Ben and Kathy Doerge, Merrie Greene French, Gary and Tina Gukeisen, Jack and Anne Milnes, Mark and Shawn Smith, Mary Catherine Smith, Karen Weight.

For those of you who read the original manuscript and gave me valuable feedback, thank you.

Special thanks goes to Gary Gukeisen for cover design and book format. The illustrations are by Robert Weller.

PROLOGUE

It is my hope that The Life-giver will encourage you. Those who desire to know God, who long for God, are indeed fortunate, for that yearning is a precious gift from the Holy Spirit who alone allows us to apprehend the things of God. I share concepts and experience with you, my readers, to facilitate a "seeing" of God in the bittersweet of ordinary life. Our common everyday situations are used by God to form in us the character of Christ. In this day and age, it is difficult to maintain hope and faith amidst the fragmentation of relationships, the religious cynicism, and the lawlessness of our culture. Often it remains unclear what God is doing, or what He wants. The unspoken struggles and battles of those who seek to obey God are shared in The Life-giver. It is in the inner soul of man that God's purpose and plan must be clearly seen.

The truth in The Life-giver is profound, and yet often not experienced. The flow of this book is not cognitive but spiritual. Read carefully and ask the Holy Spirit to allow you to see and hear what the Lord is doing and saying. The process of God's transforming power, wonderful and yet painful, is forthrightly and pragmatically presented. If you catch even a glimpse into the spiritual realm it will pique your curiosity and capture your attention. You then will look for God in everyday life and find Him pouring out His Life and Love.

My ministry has been a gracious gift from the Lord. He made Himself known to me in my earliest years. My public ministry of teaching flows out of a love for contemplation, study, and quietness. For thirty years I have helped others to deepen their "knowing" of the Lord. It is out of intimacy with the Lord that all relationships are strengthened. It has been my sacred honor to be invited into the wounded fearful inner lives of some of my friends. Over and over again I have seen the Lord enter and transform deep pain and despair with His Love. To hear Him in the quietness of my spirit, to see Him in the strength of the Word, to watch Him transform others with His Word and Spirit is my highest privilege. Participation in the mystery of His magnificent Life and Love is my delight. I honestly share some wonderful insights and also painful moments of struggle. I humbly invite you to read how the Lord makes an ordinary person like myself into a Life-giver.

5

TO THE INTERCESSORS
WHO HAVE PRAYED FOR ME FOR YEARS
THROUGH THICK AND THIN
THROUGH HELL AND HIGH WATER
THROUGH CELEBRATION AND JOY
THROUGH TEMPTATION AND STRUGGLE
THROUGH GROWING UP INTO MATURITY...
HIDDEN SAINTS
IN GRATITUDE!

THINGS
OF GOD

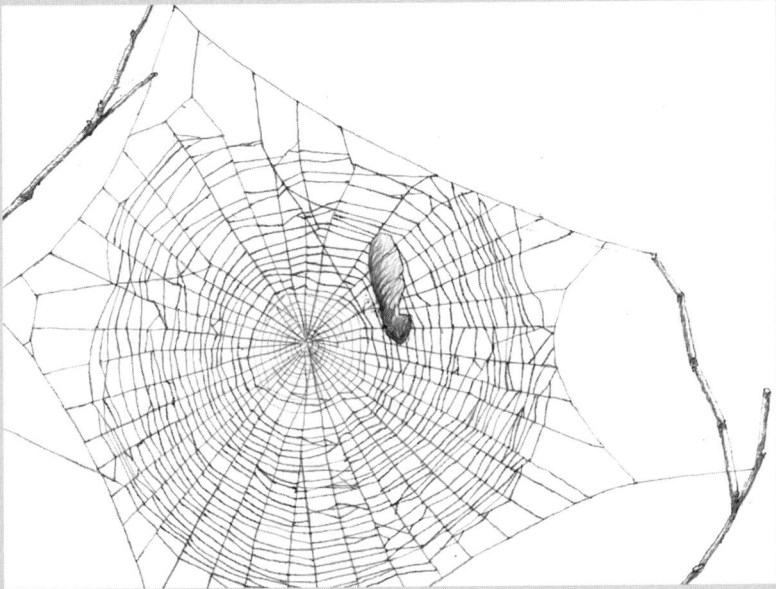

Jesus prays the night of His betrayal:
"Father, it's time.
Display the bright splendor of your Son
So the Son in turn may show your bright splendor.
You put him in charge of everything human
So he might give real and eternal life to all in his charge.
And this is the real and eternal life:
That they know you,
The one and only true God,
And Jesus Christ, whom you sent.
I glorified you on earth
By completing down to the last detail
What you assigned me to do.
And now, Father, glorify me with your very own splendor,
The very splendor I had in your presence
*Before there was a world." (Jn.17:1-5) ***

A G E N D A
O F   G O D

"This is the real and eternal life: That they may know You, the only true God, and Jesus Christ, whom you sent!" (Jn.17:3)

What does it mean to *know* the only true God? How does this *knowing* bring transformation? A word portrait, a parable, might help you, my reader, *hear and see.* A parable is a story with one central truth. Jesus told many parables. Some thought the message pointless; others clearly *heard.* The parable, *The Rich Man and a Beggar,* illustrates the contrast between ordinary human life and abundant Life. Unstop the ears!   Listen!   Turn!   See! Does the rich man *know* the Lord?   Does the beggar have Life? What is a Life-giver? How does he (she) differ from others?

THE RICH MAN AND A BEGGAR

My Rich Friend
This dignified joyful man did not appear particularly wealthy. He wore faded pants and soft, old plaid shirts patched on the elbows. Everything about him was comfortable and had a quality of permanence. He was fashionable in a way, a bit classy, yet nothing about him was new, stiff or scratchy. Even his car was worn but comfortable.

This highly successful, busy businessman was important in his field of expertise. The key to his success was his keen regard for his employees. He skillfully matched personality and training to an appropriate job. People were never sacrificed to finish the task at hand. Each person was of interest to him. He listened with concern and kindness; soon their tragedy or good news tumbled out. A light touch of the hand conveyed his thought and care. His comments were filled with wisdom. He remained the same in grocery store, home, workplace, shop, school, church.

He loved music. You could often hear him softly whistling a favorite tune. His songs reflected his inner quietness and gentle joy. Sometimes the melody was melancholy for it expressed the sorrow of a man who had lived through personal tragedy. A Bach fugue, George Winston's *Summer*, jazz and gospel delighted him.

Time was his friend. He made opportunity to sit, think, read, and meditate. He always had questions. "Lord, what do You mean by this?" "What is the truth you are showing me?" "What is my part, Father?" He cherished scriptural truth and applied it to his life. The Lord filled him with wisdom and joy during these quiet times.

He loved to hike in the rugged canyons behind his house. He donned hiking boots, rain gear, whistled for the dog, and away he went to surprise the wild critters: the deer, elk, raccoon, and rabbits. He watched the hawk ride the wind currents like a sailboat tacking across the bay. A big black beetle scurrying across the road arrested his attention. He loved each season of the year: the smell of cedar in the summer, the sweet blackberries of fall, the easy walking trails of winter, the waterfalls of spring. He listened intently to the Lord who answered his questions on these walks.

Content and thankful He knew how to rest, to quit. Sabbath for Him was a time to quiet down and remember the marvelous work of God, a time to be thankful. He knew the Lord, the God who IS. This joyful man taught me to live, *to be*. Our times together were joyful, filled with fun and delight. I became rich just being with him.

My Impoverished Friend
My other friend looked extremely chic in her tailored suit, silk blouse, beautiful scarf, and just the right shoes and hosiery. She

rose very early to exercise, shower, and organize her hectic schedule. After a forty-five minute drive to work, she arrived early to tidy up the office, setup for a business meeting, and make the coffee. She worked non-stop all during the day except during the lunch hour when she took the car in for an oil change and went to the bank. Hurried phone calls were made during her drive home. A quick stop at the grocery store facilitated dinner preparation. After dinner she rinsed the dishes and started the laundry. She then was off to the monthly meeting of the library board. An affectionate hug and quick kiss for hubby was her final good deed for the day. She did many things very well.

Driven by well doing, my friend could never rest. Yes, she was very tired yet accepted this. "That's just life," she said. The phone never stopped ringing with requests. "Could you bring refreshments, Friday?" "We are moving next Saturday, could you help?" "Would you organize a fund raiser for the school?" She volunteered, "Of course, I can do that for you!" People could count on her; she always did more than her share.

Everyone knew her at church. She attended Women's Bible Study and taught Sunday School. She cheerfully greeted each person. "Nice to see you!" "How are the kids?" "Good sermon, wasn't it?" "We'll have to get together sometime." However, she seldom heard the reply to her quick questions. When asked, "How are you doing?" She quickly answered, "Everything is great!" Her prayers were sincere and fervent, "Lord, our neighbor needs a job; heal my friend! Save my husband!"

She loved the Lord, however, something was wrong. She knew what she should be, and yet, no matter how hard she tried, it was not good enough. "I'll do better!" she vowed.

Tired and forgetful, she tried many techniques to improve her efficiency. She pounced upon new ideas and magically imagined the end product. "Of course we can do it! It will be wonderful! Just wonderful!"

It was impossible for her to read because she fell asleep in the attempt. She wanted a vacation. There was never a convenient time. Her husband wanted to have children, but how could she fit that in?

She agonized, "What is wrong! I remember being happy, now I don't feel anything. I'm just going through the motions." Afraid and bone weary, she kept going by sheer will power, short circuiting, sputtering, and then firing up again. And so this friend of mine became poorer and poorer, more and more confused and frantic, exhausted and depressed.

She never received the abundant gifts given to her — the love of others, the answers to prayer, the wisdom of the gentle quiet ones, the rest and riches of the Sabbath of the Lord, the joy of the word spoken to her by the Spirit. She had no storehouse of wisdom. She never knew time as a friend, people as reflectors of God, quiet contemplation as God's program for strengthening her. Although she was very busy and seemed very important, she, in fact, was a diminishing entity. Finally, she did not even feel the fatigue.

* * *

These two friends represent us all. Are you rich? Or are you impoverished? Perhaps, if the truth be known, at different times, you could be either, and so could I.

The first man loves God, loves himself, and loves others. He is rich, indeed. His inner heart is open. All the events of his life are the matrix in which God the Father transforms him into the image of Jesus the Son. His life exhibits the Life-giver. (For those of you who are trying to figure out who the rich man is, he is a composite of many who live in the Lord's peace and joy.)

My other friend is poverty stricken. All she seeks vanishes from her. Her man-made image of herself, an idol, demands perfection. Although a good person, all her effort brings no change. She is a captive to a distorted picture of her destiny. The Lord weeps for her whom He loves. She represents those who fail to find His rest and joy.

Jesus longs to bring Life to His bride, the Body of Christ. However she often runs to and fro doing so much yet unable to perceive the Lord in ordinary life.

* * *

Just like the gentle, joyful man, we are to be Life-givers — those who give Life. For us to change, from those who take from

11

others, to those who give life, God must totaly change us to be like Jesus. Transformation is the messy, painful process where a loving God forcefully uses all of ordinary life to press the believer into the image of His Son. All our successes, failures, stops, and starts are used by God to bring change. This destiny is not about tasks to perform or rules to follow. The significance of this destiny is beyond measure. A Forerunner, One who was the Life-giver, shows the way.

Come, join me in this quest for Life. The plan began before the beginning, *our* beginning that is. It began with God. Our first lesson defines the plan and agenda. Understanding this plan and the process of transformation is extremely important. If you decide to come along, you, a Life-giver, join many others in the greatest pursuit of a Life-time. Enamored with God, you will see the Lord change you into the image of His Son.

* * *

All Life Begins With God
Life has always existed in the intimate presence of God the Father and God the Son. It is their nature to give Life, abounding Life, glorious, marvelous Life. The Father and the Son are Life-givers. God loves to give — Life.

God the Life-giver created everything, wondrous unimaginable things: archangels, eternal realms, galaxies, stars and planets, ten thousands times ten thousand of them. He also created the tiniest of things. The better our tools for observing this vast universe inside a single cell, the more we see perfect order. The Creator must have an unlimited imagination. Even the common worm, or the graceful birds, or the reptiles reflect genius in their extraordinary display of design and color. Have you looked at the orange and black woolly caterpillar with the white whiskers? Or have you seen the red tail hawk fan his tail of muted colors of the gray, brown and red as he circles overhead? Have you listened to the loud singing of the tiny green tree frog with black eyes and golden iridescent stripes? All created life is beyond wonderful and speaks of a Creator beyond anything imaginable.

The Plan Of God
Of course, we, the image bearers of God, created to reflect and show forth our Creator, are part of creation. "Man is a spiritual

being who is not only body, but also soul and spirit. He is a moral being whose intelligence, perception, and self-determination far exceed that of any other earthly being." 1   After forming this new creature from clay, God breathed His very breath (*nishmat chay-im*)2 into Adam. His image bearer came alive. God shared with Adam His wisdom and knowledge. There was a wonderful tree in this place where Adam lived, called the Tree of Life. Its fruit was eternal Life.(Gen. 3:22) The image bearer of God was commanded to multiply and fill the earth with Life.

> Adam and Eve contained Life, the breath of God.
> Adam and Eve received wisdom
> as they communed with God.
> Adam and Eve were to have Eternal Life.
> Adam and Eve were to multiply and fill the earth
> with the very Life of God.

However, for this plan to function, Adam and his helpmate had to depend on God for everything. Both chose to turn from God, the One who is Life. Disconnected from God, they died. Death became part of the human tragedy. However, God's plan remained the same. The One who is Life set in motion actions that would bring His Life back to the descendants of Adam.

The Agenda Of God
The First Item — The Father Revealed The Son!
The verb reveal means: to draw back the veil. Unless God makes it possible, we are unable to see Him. "No man has ever seen God at any time; *the only unique Son*, or the only begotten God, Who is in the bosom, in the intimate presence, of the Father."
(Jn.1:18 Amp.) In the invisible realm the Son is so magnificent it is difficult to describe Him. He is without dimension of quality, quantity, existence, energy, passion. He is Love. Within that love exists truth and wholeness (holiness). His holiness flows outward as mercy and grace, righteousness and blessing. Everything that is needed for Life is contained in the Son. For the Father to send the Son to earth, and for us to even endure His glorious presence, the Father had to separate the Son from the invisible realm and make Him visible. The revelation of the Son is a continuous process. God revealed Himself long before Jesus came as a man. The Old Testament is a history of this revelation. Time and time again God taught the descendants of Abraham, Isaac, and Jacob. He made

13

covenants with them, kept His word, and performed miracles on their behalf. Step by step this small tribe of people learned about the One true God.

The Second Item — The Father Gave The Son!
Jesus the Son came to earth. Before His public ministry began, the Holy Spirit, John the Baptist, and God the Father declared Him to be the Messiah, the Lamb of God.

> The Holy Spirit descended upon Him. (Mk.1:10)
> John the Baptizer cried out, "Behold the Lamb of God!"
> (Jn.1:29)
> The Father declared, "This is my beloved Son!" (Lk.3:22)

To those who welcomed Him, He supplied "fullness of Life, abundance...one grace after another, spiritual blessing upon spiritual blessing, favor upon favor, gift heaped upon gift" (Jn.1:16 Amp.) They saw the glory of the Father manifested by the Son. The Apostle John tells of this:

> We heard it with our own ears, saw it with our own eyes, verified it with our own hands. The Word of Life appeared right before our eyes....The Infinite Life of God himself took shape before us. We are telling you so you too can experience it along with us, this experience of communion with the Father and his Son, Jesus Christ. Our motive for writing is simply this: We want you to enjoy this, too. Your joy will double our joy! 3

Even though the witnesses clearly announced Jesus, those wishing to remain in their own darkness could not recognize Him. They were unable to obtain Life for they did not want to know the Father or the one the Father sent. Just as Adam and Eve turned from God, these also remained independent.

The Third Item — The Son Gave His Life
I watched as a maple seed caught on a spider's web seemed to dance in the sunlight of a Fall day. The rhythmic twirling, swaying-pod of life, because it was trapped in the web, would not be able to give life.

...unless a seed falls into the ground and dies, it remains alone...

14

Jesus used this analogy of the seed to delineate the next item of the agenda of God. Jesus contained the Life of God. He came to earth to die, and like a seed, was placed into the Earth. From the Seed, resurrection Life came forth. The living Seed, filled with eternal life, planted into the dying planet, provided Life once again, for there was no living seed upon the earth. * Jesus spoke about His coming death when He said, "The hour has come that the Son of Man should be glorified. Most assuredly, I say to you, unless a grain of wheat falls into the ground and dies, it remains alone; but if it dies, it produces much grain." (Jn.12:24-25)

Jesus' death was not because of His own sin for He had never turned away from the Father. As the Life-giver, He offered His Life as a sacrifice. A living seed covered over with dirt, sprouts and becomes a plant which in turn produces much seed. Jesus, the living seed of God, overcame death as He, who is Eternal Life, came out of the grave. Jesus was victorious over death because it is impossible to destroy, crush, or eliminate His Life.

The Fourth Item — God Indwelled Those Who Believed
Belief in Jesus, the risen Christ, connected man to the source of Life. Life was now transferable to those who believed. "And this is real and eternal life: That they know you, the one and only true God, and Jesus Christ, whom you sent." (Jn.17:3) The believers received Life as "He breathed on them, and said to them, 'Receive the Holy Spirit.'" (Jn.20:19) The Father, Son and Holy Spirit entered those who welcomed Him. He gave the privilege, the authority, and the power to become the children of God. These believers were the first of a new race, children of God.

The Fifth Item — Life Multiplied
Believers, inhabited by God, contained Life. The manifested presence of the Lord increased with the addition of each believer. Revelation continued as God the Holy Spirit opened to these new believers heavenly things. The glorious Son, and the heavenly Father were seen and made known. Now God's creative power flowed from the believers causing many more to believe.

These believers, filled with Life, gathered as a corporate expression of the Life of God. He was visibly present in this corporate organism called the body of Christ, the beloved of the Lord, as

15

they reflected and magnified God. They were grafted into the Tree of Life. "I am the vine, you are the branches. He who abides in Me, and I in him, bears much fruit; for without Me you can do nothing."(Jn.15:5)   Nourished on the fruit of the tree of Life, Eternal Life, they lived in God as He flowed through them, around them, and between them, and out from them.

God accomplishes His original plan. Just as God intended for Adam and Eve, we now come into the plan God had in the beginning:

We contain the Life of God.
We receive Godly wisdom as we commune with Him.
We have eternal Life.
We multiply and express that Life.

We are Life-givers who know God who loves to give Life, and Life, and LIFE.

You did not choose Me, but I chose you and appointed you that you should go and bear fruit, and that your fruit should remain, that whatever you ask the Father in My name He may give you. (Jn.15:16)

These things I have spoken to you that My joy may remain in you, and that your joy may be full. (Jn.15:11)

THINGS
OF GOD

*"From that time Jesus began to show to His disciples that He
must go to Jerusalem and suffer many things from the elders
and chief priests and scribes, and be killed, and be raised the
third day. Then Peter took Him aside and began to rebuke Him,
saying, "Far be it from You, Lord; this shall not happen to You!"
But He turned and said to Peter, "Get behind Me, Satan! You are
an offense to Me, for you are not mindful of the things of God,
but the things of men." (Mt. 16:21-23)*

The Things of God are profound yet uncomplicated. The Father
gave the Son. Jesus revealed Himself so that all could know and
love the Father. Jesus introduced Himself as the God who *Is*, the *I
AM.* Ask yourself as you read about Him, "Have I experienced Him
as He *Is*? If you have, then you will know the Father also.

> We look at this Son and see the God who cannot be seen.
> We look at this Son and see God's original purpose in
> everything created. For everything, absolutely everything,
> above and below, visible and invisible, rank after rank after
> rank of angels — everything got started in him and finds
> its purpose in him. He was there before any of it came
> into existence and holds it all together right up
> to this moment. 1_

Jesus introduced Himself as the Messiah. It was prophesied centuries before that Messiah would do the miraculous; His actions and words spoke for themselves. Many came to Him for healing and deliverance. He taught with wisdom beyond natural understanding. He gave sight to the blind, embraced and healed the leprous, raised the dead and calmed the storms at sea. When challenged by the Pharisees, He confronted them with truth. He delivered those possessed by demons. He fed the thousands from five loaves and two fishes. Jesus met their desperate needs. He was a *Gift-giver*.

However, He, not His miracles and power, is the Gift from the Father. The purpose of the gifts, the miracles, was "to reveal the one and only true God, and the Christ, whom the Father sent." (Jn. 17:3) *

Each time Jesus touched people, He imparted His Life, as well as gifts of healing, deliverance, or wisdom. He was not just a *Gift-giver*; He was the *Life-giver*. When He healed the ten leprous men, one returned to give Him thanks. Jesus wished the others had come also to receive His blessing. (Lk. 17:17) The woman who touched the hem of His garment encountered Jesus because He did not let her secretly touch Him and then escape back into isolation. He drew her into the open, questioned and encouraged her, then healed her. As He poured His Life into others He showed forth the Father's love.

Jesus reached into the vernacular lives of people to introduce Himself. He proclaimed: *"I AM!"* *"Most assuredly, I say to you, before Abraham was, I AM." (Jn.8:58) "I AM!"* This declaration brought such a violent reaction that His listeners tried to stone Him to death. His claim to be the "I AM" disallowed their opinions. They thought of Him as just a good teacher, a good person, or someone with great giftedness. He claimed to be God, not a god; not a god promising future things, not a god for them to use. No, *He is the I AM!* Most of my readers are familiar with these scriptures and believe that Jesus is all He claimed to be. The question remains: Have you met the *I AM?* Jesus stands right in front of you and says, "Hello, my name is I AM and I am —

> *the Good Shepherd who cares for the sheep. (Jn. 10:11,14)*
> *the Door to the sheep fold (Jn. 10:7,9)*
> *the Way. (Jn. 14:6)*

18

the Truth. (Jn.14:6)
the Life. (Jn.14:6)
the Resurrection. (Jn.11:25)
the Light of Life. (Jn.8:12)
the Bread of Life." (Jn.6:48)

* * *

I AM — The Good Shepherd Who Cares For The Sheep
In Ezekiel, the coming of God as the great shepherd leader was foretold,

> Indeed I Myself will search for My sheep and seek them out...I will seek what was lost and bring back what was driven away, bind up the broken and strengthen what was sick...(Ez. 34:16)

The common life of shepherd and sheep illustrated Jesus' deep care. He sought and found the broken and sick. The loving and tender heart of the Father is also that of a shepherd.

> I will establish one shepherd over them...And I, the Lord, will be their God, and My servant David a prince among them; I the Lord, have spoken. (Ez.34:23-24)

Beloved, do you know God, the Shepherd? The One who gathers, feeds, heals, strengthens, loves you? Can you testify? "When I was abandoned and alone, Jesus, my Lord, came and gathered me into His loving care. He was my strength when I was weak and confused."

I AM — The Door To The Sheep Fold
The sheep fold was an encircled area where the sheep stayed during the night or in storms. The shepherd protected the sheep from escape and malicious intruders as he reclined across the threshold of this enclosed area. Jesus is the entrance to this place of rest, shelter and safety. All must encounter Him as he guards and protects the flock. He is the great Protector. The Father, hidden in the unseen realm, protects His loved ones as well. Have you encountered the Door? Do you know Him as the Father, who hides you from the tormentors, or as the Protector, who watches for you in the night hours while you rest?

19

I AM — The Way

The Way, is not how to get some place, or know something, or learn how to do something. Jesus here spoke about his dominion and his role in that domain. "No one comes to the Father, but by me."(Jn.14:6) He is not a way to succeed, to have victory, to be healed, to have power, to possess things. *He is the way to the Father*. There is no other way to progress from where we are to where God is, except Christ. Jesus does not teach the way; He is the Way to the Father. Jesus is God's gift. Jesus has only one person to reveal; He is the Father. This is the essence of the Things of God. Has Jesus taken you to the Father, Abba (Daddy) God?

I AM — The Truth

How would you like the person, Truth, absolute and perfect truth, to stand in front of you? Someday He will. Jesus not only speaks truth, He is Truth. Many times we search for theological knowledge to find absolute reality. We scrutinize the law of God to know His will. Jesus has a different approach to truth. He simply states that if we know Him, the I AM, "we will know the Truth, and the Truth will set us free."(Jn.8:32) We do not have to go to school and be unusually intelligent. We do not need to remember great volumes of information. We just need to know Him, the Truth who is all wisdom, knowledge, intelligence, law. Have you encountered Truth? Have you embraced deeper and deeper levels of truth? If so, then you will know God and see yourself as He sees you.

I AM — The Life

Jesus the Son is the source and reason for all Life. He is not the way to Life; He is not an idea; He is not a sometimes necessity. He is vital to man. Disconnected from Him, man is without Life, without an enlightened mind. Independent from God, a human is limited by his own strength and niftiness. Have you experienced God's Life flowing in you and out of You?

I AM — The Resurrection

"What is resurrection? Resurrection is something that has gone into death and has emerged in life. Resurrection presupposes death. There can be no resurrection where there has been no death." 2 Death entered the human race when Adam disbelieved God. We all die, an obvious fact. Jesus died as all men do. However, He had the power to emerge from death into life, resurrection life. That kind of Life is transferable into those who believe. Resurrection is beyond human ability. He is Resurrection — a thing of God! Have you been resurrected after you have suffered irreparable damage to your soul?

I AM — The Light
"I AM the light of the world: he that follows me shall not walk in darkness but shall have the light of life."(Jn.8:12) Jesus, Himself, is the Light. His words, His actions, His judgments shed light on events. His presence transforms the darkness inside the human soul. In the Gospel of John, the story of the woman caught in adultery precedes this scripture about light. Men exposed the woman's sin. Jesus instead touched her with His mercy, His truth, His command. She encountered Him and His great love. Jesus mirrored the Father, and as a consequence, she experienced the Father's love. The Father illumined the hidden shame within; His love provided forgiveness and healing. Has the Light that illumines all darkness within you, brought you to the end of yourself?

> The Light of life incapacitates the natural man by its blinding blaze and thus makes a way for God to get His purpose through. 2

I AM — The Bread Of Life
"He who comes to me will never hunger!" (Jn.6:35) "Unless you eat the flesh of the Son of Man and drink His blood, you have no life..."(Jn.6:53) "My flesh is food indeed, and My blood is drink. He who eats My flesh and drinks My blood abides in Me, and I in him." (Jn.6:56) Again Jesus reached beyond human thought into the Things of God and told them that God was to indwell them. His Life within would spiritually feed those who believe. This is a revolutionary idea, shocking to us and to the first to hear this, so offensive that many departed, not to follow Him. The natural man could not conceive of this, an indwelling God, another of those Things of God. How long has it been since you have been brimful with the Bread of Life?

* * *

The Things of God are a revelation of God the Father, God the Son, and God the Spirit.

21

The I AM is always present. Why is it frequently hard to experience Him? Some of the answers to this question are in the next section of this book, *The Things of Man*. The third and fourth sections, identify where He is, what He does, and how He does it. In addition, two simple principles may help you to know Him in your ordinary life.

Do Not Separate The Action Of God From God
We must not split the gifts from the Life-giver. If we seek Him for spiritual things, we often receive the gift, yet do not embrace Him.

> Today we pray for this thing, tomorrow for that thing, and the next day for something else. The things prayed for keep increasing; but even if the things received keep pace with the things requested, they never fully meet the need. In the purpose of God, Christ is not only the Giver of everything we need; *He is everything we need.* It is a recognition of this that produces vital Christianity in contrast to Christianity as it is commonly conceived with its stress on externalities. 3

Have you been able to sustain faith, hope, love, healing, patience, kindness, blessing? Most of us find it difficult. God designs it that way! God designs it that way so that we come to Him. The loss of spiritual things continues until we embrace the Source. No matter how much He loves to give the gifts, He so much more wants the gift, the thing, to be a symbol of Himself. He gives us Life which includes all spiritual things. This Life is everlasting, eternal, undiminished, forever.

Do Not Separate God From Everyday Life
God must not be isolated into religious life. Is it a duty to "spend a little time with Jesus?" If we only relate to Him during these times, He is excluded from most of the day. God may be ignored until something is needed. A quick "I need" prayer is like a phone call to God, quite similar to the call from the college kid. "Hey Dad how are you? Great, glad to hear it. By the way I'm running a little short of cash. Suppose you could send a few bucks? Thanks! See ya." If this be true, normal, daily life has nothing to do with God. Our life is compartmentalized into ordinary life and religious life.

So how do we overcome this problem? The answer is simple, so simple it is often missed. How does it work? Talk to Him about everything. Instead of talking to yourself in your thoughts, talk to Him. You think, *"He cannot be interested in all the minute details of my life. God's in heaven running the universe, separated from unimportant man."* This attitude is incorrect. Even human parents are interested and love each of their children. Human love multiplies to embrace each child. It enlarges to encompass each. It also individuates so that particular child is loved differently from any others. If humans can love, God certainly is able to do the same. He can love individually, perfectly and with great interest. No life is superfluous; all life is precious. A gift of a wilted dandelion from a child is a delight to the mother. Do you really think that God despises our conversation?

He is part of our ordinary day when we communicate with Him. It is then possible to sense His immediate presence and become aware of His joy over little things or His sadness over the plight of life. He might even give us new ideas and thoughts. The inner communion might sound like this:

> *"Good morning Lord, thanks for the rest. I'm not ready to face the day. Please be my strength. Thanks for putting up with me. Did you see the smile on Suzy's face when she put her shoes on by herself? This family is sure great. Thanks. That person on the bus sure looks troubled. Lord touch him. Thanks for giving me the solution to the engineering problem while I was out on lunch break. Joe has been so crabby lately, please help him. Show me how to encourage him. What does it mean to wait on you?...."*

He loves to answer your questions. He is there to bring understanding to the Things of God. Ask Him, then listen. Have you asked Him about His concerns? Or how He sees things? Our fellowship with Him deepens as He is included in everyday life.

Do not split the gifts from the Source.
>> He is the Gift.
>> He is Life.

Do not put God in a box called "out there."
>> He lives inside believers.
>> Acknowledge His presence. He is everywhere!

The only thing God gives to us is Jesus. He is all there is of the Things of God. Jesus has only one person to reveal, the Father. This is the essence of the Things of God.

>> Now we have received, not the spirit of the world, but the Spirit who is from God, that we might know the things that have been freely given to us by God. (ICor.2:12)

NOTES

Section 1
Things of God
* Eugene Peterson, *The Message,* (Colorado Springs, Colorado: Navpress, 1993), p. 223 I have chosen to use this edition of the New Testament because of its paraphrase into modern language. Since we often become familiar with the more traditional translations and often miss their meaning, I am using this very excellent rendition for its shock effect.
"Jesus spoke these words, lifted up His eyes to heaven, and said: 'Father, the hour has come. Glorify Your Son, that Your Son also may glorify You, as You have given Him authority over all flesh, that He should give eternal life to as many as You have given Him. And this is eternal life, that they many know You, the only true God, and Jesus Christ whom You have sent. I have glorified You on the earth. I have finished the work which You have given Me to do. And now, O Father, glorify Me together with Yourself, with the glory which I had with You before the world was.'" (Jn. 17:1-5 NKJ)

Chapter 1
The Agenda of God
1 *Spirit Filled Life Bible New King James*, footnote "Man's Intrinsic Value," (Gen. 1:26-28) p.6
2 James Strong, *The Exhaustive Concordance Bible,*(Peabody, Mass.,Hendrichson Pub.Co.) Hebrew p.80 #5397
3 Peterson, *The Message*, p.501.
* Gene Edwards, *Divine Romance,* (Gardiner, Maine: Christian Book Publishing House, 1984) This book presents a wonderful concept of the seed from the Eternal Realm.

Chapter 2
Things of God
1 Peterson, *The Message*, p.422.
"He is the image of the invisible God, the firstborn over all creation. For by Him all things were created that are in heaven and

that are on earth, visible and invisible, whether thrones or dominions or principalities or powers. All things were created through Him and for Him. And He is before all things, and in Him all things consist." (Col.1:15-17NKJ)

* Watchman Nee, *Twelve Baskets Full, Vol. 1,* (Fort Washington, Penn. World Literature Crusade, 1969)
p. 31-43. Although the entire chapter was not used, "The Sum of Divine Things" is an excellent source. It was used for its concept.
2 Nee, *Twelve Baskets Full,* p.38.
3 Nee, *Twelve Baskets Full,* p.32.

THINGS
OF MAN

*Jesus then said, "I came into the world to bring everything
into the clear light of day, making all the distinctions clear, so
that those who have never seen will see, and those who have
made a great pretense of seeing will be exposed as blind.
"(Jn.9:37) 1*

THINGS
OF MAN

*"For what man knows the things of a man except the spirit of
the man which is in him? Even so no one knows the things of
God except the Spirit of God." (ICor.2:11)*

A man is born, toils and labors, and then dies. In a nutshell, this
describes "the Things of Man."

As I watched our boys dig a moat around a complex sand castle, I
thought how similar a sand castle is to human endeavor. The
incoming tide had, as yet, not reached the elegant fort. Our entire
family had labored for hours constructing an intricate structure
with turrets, chambers, walls, and streets. The dungeon was built
first; then the king's rooms were placed upon it. Each tier added
splendor to this imaginary castle of a fantasy king who existed for
a magical moment. Each outer wall was built carefully to keep the
'enemy' from taking the castle. The driftwood gate, fashioned by
the tumbling surf, opened and closed as directed by the masters
of this fort.

Finished at last, we stepped back to admire the three dimensional
creation. Dad had carefully build delicate layers of dripped sand
to make the spires; I had supplied sea water by the bucketful.
Our boys talked of battles and warfare. Our daughter imagined
what it would be like to be a princess.

It was a magnificent day of wonder and play.

"Quick, dig the breakwater deeper!" "Look the moat is filling with water!" "The tide is coming in!"

The boys, bored with admiring their creation, pushed and shoved each other and broke part of the wall of the castle. The incoming sea softened the foundation below the dungeon. The kids ran to fly a kite; we sat and watched. Moments later the castle crumbled into a mass of sand. An hour later the beach was smooth; no sign was left of the wonderful imaginary castle.

The day is just a memory now, a good memory,
but only a memory.

* * *

Often life seems like the day of the sand castle. We have been intent upon building a legacy, a deposit of life, that would endure. Often much of our labor ends up like the sand castle, just a memory of a special time.

We continually strive to maintain life. Each of us invests time and energy to build a life that is worthwhile. Work, family, routines, hobbies, home constitute our domain, a place where we seem to be in control. We labor to guarantee a "decent" life for our family. These are the Things of Man, not bad nor good, merely the natural flow of things.

However, natural man moves from simplicity to complexity.

Quite often when insecure in position or dominion, a man (woman) finds it necessary to prove he is important. Driven to verify his significance, he builds a complex system, 'a kingdom,' the domain of the 'i am.' He has his own law, so to speak, which is in place to keep him in power. He gathers into his realm things and people to provide support for his position and status. He must then work hard to control and to protect all his domain. Unfortunately, just like the incoming tide, circumstances are uncontrollable. Eventually, the labor of his life comes to an end. Emotional, spiritual and physical death destroys the grand scheme.

29

The Things of Man is human effort to build, gather, keep, possess and preserve things.

As bleak and inescapable as this may sound, there is another way to live. The Lord taught a path that leads to Life. We, the Life-givers, gain Life as it is given to others. We must first present our very ordinary life to the Lord.

> For whoever desires to save his life will lose it, but who-ever loses his life for My sake will save it. For what profit is it to a man if he gains the whole world, and is himself destroyed or lost. (Lk.9:24)

The principle contained in this scripture is very foreign to natural man and seems to be antithetical to well being. To control and possess is deeply ingrained in our nature. However Jesus, the first Life-giver, modeled this way of life as He gave and sacrificed.

None of us is immune from this proclivity to kingdom-build. The believer who is a Life-giver must struggle in an intense continuous battle. Do I strive to accumulate and maintain the Things of Man, or do I give life? On one hand it is natural to build and accumu-late; on the other hand it is right to freely give. When we ignore the Lord's way and strive to keep our kingdom for ourselves, we never win. Everything eventually ends in loss. Jesus told this story:

> Take care! Protect yourself against the least bit of greed. Life is not defined by what you have, even when you have a lot."Then he told them this story:"The farm of a certain rich man produced a terrific crop. He talked to himself: 'What can I do? My barn isn't big enough for this har-vest.' Then he said,'Here's what I'll do: I'll tear down my barns and build bigger ones. Then I'll gather in all my grain and goods, and I'll say to myself, Self, you've done well! You've got it made and can now retire. Take it easy and have the time of your life!' Just then God showed up and said,'Fool! Tonight you die. And your barn full of goods — who gets it?: That's what happens when you fill your barn with Self and not with God. (Lk.12) 2

If we continue the unending pursuit of our own sovereignty, we often burn out, the effort taking its toll. The symptoms of striving to retain the kingdom of 'i am' are cynicism, hopelessness, and depression. Debilitating depression and anxiety, chronic and paralyzing, become a way of life. Believers and non-believers reap a harvest of confusion and despair. The insistence upon the Things of Man separates us from the Life-giver; living death is the result.

Surprisingly enough, the Spirit of God uses this dilemma to teach us another way. The next sections of this book, *Follow Me — To Establish Foundation* and *Follow Me Into Life* present the way of the Life-giver, a way to release the old way, and embrace a totally new manner of living. The Spirit teaches us to leave behind the foolish pursuit of the Things of Man.

As a pastoral counselor, I have seen many in the burn-out stage. They bitterly cry, "Nothing I do matters; nothing will help; nothing means anything. I have no ambition." They have no mental or emotional energy left. Their kingdom has failed.

* * *

A father of one of my friends walked into my office for his first appointment. Even though intelligent, highly educated, and widely read, He had lost everything: a wife, family, career. With years of experience in the world of business and social action, self reliant and confident (even in this state of affairs), He still hoped to figure things out and run his own life. Hyperviligent and leery of me, He set me on notice saying, "There is no reason to trust you or any woman. I doubt that you can help me. I am a Christian. I've sought God all my life." As the conversation deepened, he shared his great frustration and despair. "I must admit, I have found little reality in the practice of Christianity. Personally each time I think I have found the so called reality of God, He disappears like a mirage." Untrusting and cynical, he said "I've tried counseling. I've gone to church. It is as corrupt as any other institution; everyone is out to get something. You had better not lead me on; you had better have answers. My life is essentially over. There is nothing left to value. I desperately need to find purpose for living. I'll pay any price to find God. Unless I find some answers, I will...take my life." He was at his "wits end."

I listened to his despair and loneliness and thought, *"Come, Lord Jesus. He is ready to meet you, really meet you!"* The challenge was ahead, the stakes high, the risk real. Life or death, what would it be? We began a tumultuous, exciting battle for this man's sanity and life. Would he leave behind his kingdom and find the Life-giver, and in turn become a Life-giver?

Several months later this man wrote his story and gave me a copy. He gave me permission to share it with you.

A year ago to the day — life narrowed into a blackness with no bottom. Remembering is painful for it was my own doing that brought me to that place of despair.

Let me share...

Adult men in our social system find it easy to squander decades achieving the "good life." Teen years are filled with dreams and hopes; we prepare for the great life. Those yearnings drive us to marriage, family, house, cars, education, better jobs, position in the community. As we achieve we convince ourselves we are making it .. 'just look at my achievements, lovely family, beautiful house, expensive car.' Trophies of success.

Only there comes a time when *things crack a little.* The big house, the job, the friends don't bring satisfaction. We work harder...but the wife is distant...the kids are busy. Maintaining the yard, the house, ball games, cards, hobbies, the sweetness of 'success' *now are empty of meaning. We are afraid to admit it. The decades of hav-ing our own way have taken their toll.* Our lives are dry as dust. The children also have started to seek "the good life." Friends are having affairs, drinking too much, some have died. Marriages are sterile, friends are only acquain-tances. Airports, eating out, conventions, awards are all plastic.

No one knows you and no one cares. When the kid gets cancer, friends don't know what to say. No one can stand you; the wife falls apart; you put the pain away and cope. Christmas cards — calls on birthdays, symbols of family ties, no one is close.

Work is the only thing left but that is taking it's toll — stress, change, disappointment, a lay off — time out — to think — to read. You realize you have been dead for the last decade, maybe longer. You sit, you worry, financial ruin could happen, death seems too close, the wife asks for a divorce; what a time to do that...The dreams are gone.

People die; first it was Dad, a whole life lived for what? Then a friend was killed by a teen drunk driver. That really got to you. Then your childhood friend tells you she has a ghastly melanoma growing into her brain.

I sure hope I don't lose my mind...

And so you sit, you think — you have barely escaped your own snare and delusion. You have some sanity left, some intelligence, some integrity, but what seemed so important and worthwhile is now a delusion. With little time and no energy you are certain you cannot pull off a rescue. The analyst, the counseling did not do it.

The devious pathways of your own mind lead to no answers, but something inside needs to be fixed. There is something very wrong inside the inside of your very inner mind that has a grip on you, the little addiction to the quick flashes of anger only you see, the big addiction to work, work, work. The tension, the fears creep in. A cold sweat, fear, sleepless nights...your life begins to disintegrate. Now the family who thought you were always a little nuts, says so with nice nasty comments that kill you as if a gun was fired at your mid-section at close range. The ex-wife whispers, "I told you so," to the kids. There are mad dogs everywhere.

Employment is doubtful, unemployment insurance stops — you have no money, no home, no one who cares. Depression sets its ugly teeth into you and bites hard so that black is not an adequate description. Your mind is leaving you; you know it; you can hide it sometimes, but it disintegrates on a regular schedule.

Then, there is a moment, a traumatic moment, when the littlest, most faint, most distant hope is utterly and absolutely shattered, and your entire idea of reality and sanity depart. The mind and body no longer are together. You run out into the night across fields not knowing where you are going and not caring. The pain is searing, agonizing, and you can't stand on you feet. The ground is not even noticed. It's coolness can't quench the gut wrenching, vomiting, choking, head blinding pain. In that moment you scream ——

GOD — STOP THE PAIN!

In that moment — a choice.

A choice to lay aside the citadel of your own mind which has led to this unbearable hell. Your having your own way has led you to this moment. **The choice is either to remain in the hell you have created for yourself or to ask for a new life...**

In that moment — life changed permanently.

The dark night sky turns to gray and morning finds your body covered with dew. There is not a shred of peace. Your agony remains. You remember that you have to go to work. Uncomprehending — Numb — going through the motions — not able to eat — You feel only the numbing psyche and physical pain. You loose weight. Weeks go by — however — Very slowly things start to change —

You leave your job, your east coast location — to return to your children.

You find a friend —

Suicidal plans are cut off at 2:00 AM. Instantly you know that death is not a solution.

Sleep is possible —

Slowly, slowly, slowly a small shadow of a long ago memory of a deep, peaceful, silent place enters and stays

You weep —

You feel again —

This was not of your doing; you had done nothing. Another depression, another interdiction preventing suicide. None of it your doing. And, in the slow dawning of the meaning, you realize that since the moment you made that choice, there has been a mighty hand on you. You have been taken into God's mighty hand.

He has told you to be still — to heal — to rest.

Nothing else matters — this is the place of comfort.

Tension is gone — ease has returned —

Joy sets in —

There is clarity of mind — peace.

You know without a shadow of doubt — "His Mercy Endures Forever!"

Is this man unusual in his pursuit of the good life and its cata-strophic outcome? I do not think so. It is only natural to long for comfort and security. However, this permanent sense of well-being is found *only* in God. His response to our cry, *"Oh God, Oh God...Jesus, my life is a mess...Oh God"* is to gently invade life with His Presence; we are able to receive mercy, truth, and most of all love. This process continues for an entire lifetime as He gives to us more and more of His Life. It is His joy to do so.
Life is our portion!

The opposite also is true. If we continue to pursue the Things of Man, detached from God, our natural strength determines our resources. Physical, emotional and spiritual strength diminishes with age unless we find strength from another Source. When we are independent and govern our own lives, we essentially become our own god. God warns, "If you try to be God, death is the result." Many kinds of death are possible: physical, living, emotional, intellectual.

Living Death
A sweet, beautiful fifteen year old girl thinks that Mom is a bit old fashioned. The classic argument ensues, "I want more freedom." "You will not have freedom until you show some maturity." "All I want Mom, is to spend time with Joe. He is so cute and he likes me. I'm popular with the guys on the football team. No, Mom, of course not, I'm not going to sleep with him. What's wrong with going over to his house after school? No, his parents aren't there. You don't trust me?" Unfortunately, this teen wants what she wants and does not listen. She begins the spiral downward:
>the betrayal of friends to gain that cute boy-friend.
>the moral compromise to "please" the boys.
>the lying to deceive parents about her whereabouts.
>the cheating on tests to appear successful.
>the dropping out of school.
>the entrapment of early marriage.
>the physical abuse endured because of fear.
>the use of alcohol to cover the pain.

By the age of twenty-five, this beautiful girl is a living dead per-son. Despondent and despairing, she is afraid to change her cir-cumstances. She tries to maintain the image of beauty even though her zip and vitality are gone. This is living death.

Emtional Death

The wedding is the picture of perfection. Everything, absolutely everything, is perfect! This intelligent, good looking couple vows to do everything right. "We'll not make the same mistakes as our parents. We'll work through all our problems in a civilized manner. We'll share the work load. The kids will behave and have all the right stuff. We'll go to church, teach them right, even put them into the very best private schools." However, the beauty queen gains sixty pounds in her first pregnancy. The perfect baby cries night and day. The handsome husband prefers to read the newspaper in the morning instead of chatting with the wife. The perfect kid is angry, willful and ungrateful. One night the perfect couple loses control and has a loud and hurtful fight. The kid agitates both of them. They worry. The pressure of the house payment, the endless nights up with the sick kid, the temptation of an affair with the beautiful secretary at work, the expensive new car that they cannot afford, add to the stress. The perfect image crumbles. Passionate love ebbs away. Everything appears the same, but now life is pretending. There is no more love for one another; no more joy in parenting. Everything is numb. This is emotional death.

Intellectual Death

He is in the top one percentile in the nation, a national merit scholar. College is one party after another, but his intelligence carries him through with good grades. Upon graduation he finds that job opportunities come easily. Work challenges him most of the time; there is little time for reading. He is no longer curious about anything. Work, television, the newspaper head-lines and sport page, the technical information for the job are his intellectual daily diet. The banalities of television with its jiffy news, action packed quick solution programs, and advertising promising everything, are his 'food of thought.' Literature, history, music and art have no place in his world. No longer does he feel excitement. Boredom is the menu, isolation and stagnation the routine. Intellectual exercise is as limited as the physical exercise of an invalid. This is intellectual death.

The girl, the perfect couple, the genius are dying. Death encompasses them. The motivation to work hard, learn new things and become involved with people no longer exists. No one notices their desperation. The Source of Life has been cut off; death reaps more victims.

Living, emotional, intellectual, and eventually, spiritual death can befall Christians and non-Christians alike. Our strong natural tendency to 'kingdom-build' and detach from God, is our greatest enemy. The cause of this disasterous direction is our flesh, our ego, the great "I" within all of us. Here lays the danger. We revert back to the 'i am' when we believe there is no danger of it. Our self enthronement, the exalted place, a place of personal power and influence, destroys our life with the Lord. Death automatically occurs unless we remain attached to the Life-giver.

Paul writes to the Roman Christians:

> So here's what I want you to do, God helping you: Take your everyday, ordinary life — and place it before God as an offering. Embracing what God does for you is the best thing you can do for him. Don't become so well-adjusted to your culture that you fit into it without even thinking. Instead, fix your attention on God. You'll be changed from the inside out — Living then, as every one of you does, in pure grace, it's important that you not misinterpret yourselves as people who are bringing this goodness to God. No, God brings it all to you. **The only accurate way to understand ourselves is by what God is and by what he does for us, not by what we are and what we do for him.** (Rom.12:1) 3

B O R N
B L N D

"If our Message is obscure to anyone, it's not because we're hold-ing back in any way. No, it's because these other people are looking or going in the wrong way and refuse to give it serious attention. All they have eyes for is the fashionable god of dark-ness. They think he can give them what they want, and that they won't have to bother believing a truth they can't see. They're stone-blind to the dayspring brightness of the Message that shines with Christ who gives us the best picture of God we'll ever get."
(11Cor.4:4) 1

I watched as twenty children at the city park played cops and rob-bers or good guys, bad guys. The kids crawled through tunnels, swung across a rope bridge, climbed up log towers, slid down the slide. Yelling, pushing and shoving, the children were unaware of my watchfulness and curiosity.

I was fascinated by their active play because I knew that two of the boys were legally blind. They had inherited a type of blind-ness that resulted in extreme near-sightedness and color-blindness. They could see only very large objects directly in front of them; they had no side vision. Even though they were blind, they seemed to play as if sighted. Only once did the oldest of the two run smack dab into the crossbeam of the tunnel. He stopped, rubbed his head, stretched out his hand, felt the timber, crouched down and then crawled into the tunnel. The younger brother was a bit timid at the top of the slide but when shoved by a friend, flew down the slide and landed in the sawdust at the bottom. From that time on, he was the first up the ladder and the quickest to the bottom.

How could they function so well with such limited vision? They knew nothing else. This forced them to adapt and use other senses to accomplish the task at hand. With each new experience they learned more and became confident. John, the oldest, played the piano. To locate the notes, he gently touched the two black keys, felt the half step dowr ... later he distinguished each note by sound. Tom, the y... violin. They read by holding a book ju... seem strange to them. W... with depth perception?... had never known norm... were missing. They ha... could see. However, t...

Why this story? There is a parallel in spiritual life. With... dard outside our own experience, we often think we see when in reality we are partially blind. Some things may be seen clearly while others are not. Our sight is limited, at best. Much of spiritual life may not be experienced or understood. This is not how it should be.

Spiritual Vision

What is spiritual vision? Vision is the act or power of seeing with the eye, the sense of sight. Vision includes the ability to perceive something not actually visible, through mental acuteness or keen foresight or imagination. 2

Spiritual things are invisible. The object, concept or plan must be revealed to perceive it. The verb reveal means to draw back the veil and make known something hidden. 3   God is in the business of revelation, the pulling back of the veil. The Holy Spirit is our tutor who reveals the Things of God.

It is important to understand that mankind is born spiritually blind. "Unless one is born again, he cannot see the kingdom of God." (Jn.3:3) Unbelievers often think their view of life is right, not realizing their blindness. To be physically blind is a great tragedy. How much greater the catastrophe when many in our society are spiritually blind, yet think they see. As a result, the blindness is not acknowledged and as a consequence, treatment and help are refused.

> The basic reality of God is plain enough. Open your eyes and there it is! By taking a long and thoughtful look at what God has created, people have always been able to see what their eyes as such can't see; eternal power, for instance, and the mystery of his divine being. So nobody has a good excuse. What happened was this: people knew God perfectly well, but when they didn't treat him like God, refusing to worship him, they trivialized themselves into silliness and confusion so that there was neither sense nor direction left in their lives. They pretended to know it all, but were illiterate regarding life. (Rom.1) 4

Although this certainly applies to the unbeliever, believers are not exempt. They can, and often do, lack spiritual vision.

Spiritual vision is the ability to see God in ordinary life, to discern what He is doing. God is seen as pre-eminent; man is seen as a created being. God is the center, man is rightly related to Him. In addition, life is filled with enjoyment and thanksgiving, for everything is seen as provision from the Lord. Life is colorful. The grays and blacks, the whites and neutrals, are endued with hue. Things are seen as they really are, even things in the spiritual realm. There is no confusion or blocked perception. All things are rightly seen in relationship with others. Past history is aptly applied to current events and tomorrow holds no terror. The most important things have greater priority than the unimportant. What is seen is comprehended.

We certainly would be transformed if you and I had this kind of vision. Unfortunately, we see rather poorly. Some common perceptive inaccuracies can be corrected if the distortions are identified and understood.

Vision Without Focus

If one is spiritually near-sighted, it is impossible to see beyond the things at hand, beyond ordinary life into the greater things of God. Time and energy are consumed by the crisis in the marriage, the problems at work, the constant testing of teens, or the ever present car repairs. Just to make it through a day with a cheerful attitude is a miracle. Life seems to go on pretty much the same whether there is belief in God or not. Thoughts and feelings, decisions and plans remain ours. When urgent matters are the focus, God's plan is invisible.

On the other hand, those who are far-sighted cannot see God in current circumstances. They are focused on the future. They look forward to a better day. They want to escape ordinary life and go to heaven. Many times they are consumed with anticipatory fear of an unknown future filled with catastrophe. If God is not seen today, He will be missed when the future turns into today.

This kind of visual impairment caused many people to miss Jesus. Some thought the Messiah would come in the future. Others thought He would save the nation from the Roman Empire. Few saw Him when He appeared. Just like our historical ancestors, we can miss Him too! Man has great difficulty seeing beyond the nearness of things or the anticipation of an unknown future. We can be so busy with our own world, we may never even say "Hello!" to the indwelling King.

The unfathomable depths of God do unfold when we yearn to find Him. Our spiritual acuity increases in direct proportion to an honest desire to know and to see God and His kingdom. To improve spiritual vision expect Him to accompany you at home, in the work place, on the bus ride, to the doctors visits, to school, to church, during meals, and while reading to the kids. The truly wise, the meek in spirit, the humble, see Him in sharp focus because they seek Him. Turn away from the crisis of life; turn towards Him. Stop looking at the things at hand; stop looking to the future; stop looking in the past. He is! The I AM is outside of time so He is always dwelling with us right now!

Vision Without Color

What is spiritual color-blindness? God describes this inability to see like this:

I know you inside and out, and find little to my liking.
You're not cold, you're not hot — far better to be either
cold or hot! You're stale. You're stagnant. You make me
want to vomit. You brag, 'I'm rich, I've got it made, I need
nothing from anyone,' oblivious that in fact you're a piti-
ful, blind beggar, threadbare and homeless. (Rev.3:15) 5

The word enthusiasm comes from *en,* in + *theos,* god. In other
words, enthusiasm means to be possessed by a god. The person
who is enthusiastic has a supernatural fervor, zeal, intensity. The
synonym is passion. 6   Life is filled with color, zest, vigor.

When someone is afflicted with spiritual color-blindness, life slips
into neutral. Nothing seems important or lovely. This may happen
infrequently, or, it can become a life style. When unpleasantness
becomes the main course, spiritual life ebbs away. Let me illustrate with two different examples.

When Mt. St. Helens erupted in 1980 we were affected for months
due to the ash fallout from the volcano. (We live fifty miles south-
west of the mountain.) The abrasive fine powder caused extensive
damage to power lines which frequently shorted out. As the ash
fell, the trees and flowers, animals, roads, parking lots and cars,
everything turned gray. For that entire summer it either rained
mud or it blew dense clouds of dust which lowered visibility to
zero. The ash rose into the air, seeded the clouds and then it
rained mud. The gritty powder seeped through the tinniest of
holes into the house. Everything was covered. There was no
escape. Depression and irritability describe the mood of the summer. Just like the ash, every situation was contaminated by this
emotional bleakness. I felt hopeless; I lost my zest for life. The
cyclic routines of life fed my despair. I was dull, depressed and
unthankful, and consequently, unable to see God in the situation.

I keenly recall another example of spiritual color-blindness. It was
Christmas and time for the annual Winter Program at the elemen-
tary school. My youngest of four children was singing with the
fourth grade class. My attitude was terrible and progressively
became worse. My inner thoughts escalated into a continual
stream of unhappiness. My inner murmuring went like this:

"I sure don't want to be here. For sixteen years I have come to this stupid program, and now it has deteriorated into happy Hanukkah, winter wonderland, Rudolph, and seasons greetings. Hope I don't have to talk to anyone. I'll read my book and pretend to be absorbed in the story. I even had to come alone. Sometimes life is just made to endure. I guess it is important to come for the kids..."

My stream of complaints and murmurings went on and on, just like the ash that covered everything and everybody. I had no joy, no interest in anything.

Until — A marvelous laugh, a chuckle, interrupted these miserable musings. Curious, I abandoned my inner grumbling to locate the source of this delightful laughter. At the end of the row Pastor Hutch, old and bent, chuckled with delight at the active preschoolers who were running about in the center aisle. I watched as the children came to him. He affectionately hugged and talked to them, all the while chuckling with enjoyment. As people passed by, he inquired about their latest news and nodded and smiled as they shared with him.

The program finally started as first graders tripped onto the stage decked out in white stocking caps. The boys pulled the girl's hair. Some kids yelled, "Hi, Mom," and waved at friends and family. An elbow in the side of the talkative ones from a quiet member of the class brought the waving to a stop. Pastor Hutch clapped for joy as they sang "Rudolph the Red-nose Reindeer." As the program continued, Hutch hummed along to "Winter Wonderland" and "Frosty the Snowman." Waving and laughing, exuding joy, he loved every minute of it. The entire community joined all the kids in the singing of "Silent Night." As he sang of the birth of his beloved Savior, this dear saint of God, who had walked with Jesus for over fifty years, wept.

By this time I saw the contrast between an *enthusiast*, one possessed by God, and one who is color-blind. I was forever ashamed. I, who call myself a Christian, had put God into a tiny box and let the gray bleakness of self-pity possess me. It is possible to live without vim and vigor, bored and unthankful, in a darkness of our own making. Unfortunately, this mood spreads to others.

43

An attitude of joy can also spread. When I witnessed God's joy and love pouring through Pastor Hutch, I immediately saw the deficiency in my own behavior. I had not enjoyed this event because I had pulled the shade across my spiritual eyes and descended into a dark basement. When we trudge through life whining and griping, unaware of others, life turns gray. The color fades away until there are only the blacks and grays, the dark shades of despair.

In contrast, Jesus spoke about His joy, "These things I have spoken to you, that My joy may remain in you, and that your joy may be full." (Jn.15:11) Jesus came to take us from this darkness, add bright color, the infinite brilliance of His Life. The Holy Spirit joins us as a companion, to point out occasions of joy and life. Our journey parallels Jesus' life. He enjoyed life; we read of His zeal, His passion. He was a man filled with God. He was God filled with love and joy. Here is His command:

> Here's what I want you to do: Buy your gold from me, gold that's been through the refiner's fire. Then you'll be rich. Buy your clothes from me, clothes designed in Heaven. You've gone around half-naked long enough. And buy medicine for your eyes from me so you can see, *really* see. The people I love, I call to account, prod and correct and guide so that they'll live at their best. Up on Your feet, then! About face! Run after God! (Rev.3:15-20)7

Vision Without Clarity
The spiritual realm is not clearly seen. Paul describes this, "For now we see in a mirror, dimly, but then face to face." (1 Cor. 13:12) This ancient mirror made of unpolished metal, reflected only a dim image. To illustrate further, it is impossible to see clearly through a very dirty windowpane. Eugene Peterson, in *The Message*, renders this analogy as "peering through fog." This aptly describes hazy spiritual vision. Our youngest son used to say, "Let's go jugging in the frog." What he meant to say was, "Let's go jogging in the fog!" Think for a moment how jogging in fog describes perfectly how we see with unclear spiritual vision. While jogging in fog much energy is expended; health may be achieved. We return to our starting point with a sense of well-being. We have run energetically, with great vigor, in a huge circle. Although we passed wondrous sights and vistas, the blowing mist blocked our vision. There may have been marvelous sights to enjoy, but

unless God burns off the fog, we never see them. Sounds much like some of my spiritual experiences. How about yours?

One day this dim vision will lift and we will see God face to face. There have been awesome, extraordinary, and terrifying times when God has removed the veil and man has seen some of the spiritual realm.

God appeared to the people of Israel. They witnessed the thundering, the lighting flashes, the sound of the trumpet, and the mountain smoking; and when the people saw it, they trembled and stood afar off. Then they said to Moses, "You speak with us, and we will hear; but let not God speak with us, lest we die." "So the people stood afar off, but Moses drew near the thick darkness where God was. (Ex.20:18-19,21)

The prophet Isaiah saw the spiritual realm where God was high and lifted up, holy and awesome. The prophet cried out, "Woe is me, for I am undone!...For my eyes have seen the King, the Lord of hosts!" (Is.6:5)

Paul related, "how he was caught up into Paradise and heard inexpressible words, which it is not lawful for a man to utter. (IICo.12:4)

John, the Apostle, said, "And when I saw Him, I fell at His feet as dead." (Rev.1:17)

Maybe it is a good thing that our vision of the spiritual realm is unclear. It may be for our protection and comfort.

When someone is over confident in their ability to see into the spiritual realm, their opinions sound like this: "God is like this!" "God will do that!" "The second coming of Christ will be...!" "He wouldn't act like that!" "Let me tell you what God thinks of you!" "I see demons and you have a spirit of ..." "Haven't you seen your angel yet? He is right beside you." (For those lacking the ability to see angels, it might be good to keep Balaam's Ass, or one like it, around to let you know when an angel is afoot!) (see Nu.22:33)

Seriously, the scriptures are the revelation of God. Jesus is the best picture of God we will ever see. There is always more to learn of

Him. God is present both in the word and in the witness of the Christ-bearers. However, the totality of God remains veiled until the final events in history. When He comes, we will see Him clearly and totally. Until that time, we see with diminished vision.

Vision Without Perspective

Perspective means *per,* through + *specere,* to look, to look through. 8   When an object is drawn on a blank sheet of paper separated from other objects, it is impossible to tell its size, location, or importance. A tree can be small or large, close or far away, important or unimportant when viewed alone. Placed into the scene, the tree then is properly related to everything else.

If life is to be understood, it must be seen in correct perspective. In reality everything in the universe centers upon God. * It is as if God is a giant gear. Jesus, the Son, enmeshed in this gear, turns in harmony with God, the Father. Everything else turns upon the Son to accomplish the Father's plan. Everything comes into perspective when Jesus is acknowledged as all important.

Without this perspective, man thinks he is the center of the universe, and God is on the periphery. Man then assumes that God, like a servant, is to fit his plans. When God does not hop to and wait on us, anger results. Stop and think about this. How often do we expect God to obediently obey our commands? Unless the Christian matures beyond self-centeredness, God is not seen. Life seems eccentric, out of round. Nothing quite works. The gears are independent from God and turn round and round but accomplish nothing.

When God is preeminent, then man finds his place.

> When I consider Your heavens, the work of Your fingers,
> The moon and the stars, which You have ordained,
> What is man that You are mindful of him,
> And the son of man that You visit him?
> For You have made him a little lower than the angels,
> And You have crowned him with glory and honor.
> You have made him to have dominion over the works of Your hands;
> You have put all things under his feet. (Ps.8:3-6)

46

When man is the standard it is necessary to measure oneself against other men. We hear the comparisons constantly, "I am better than you!" "He is wealthy; they are poor." She sure is lucky; they are unfortunate." Wealth, talent, intelligence, physical strength and beauty are premium traits. The infirm old, the single parent, the unborn child, the 'foreigner' are of less value. Please note! This rating system is wrong and flawed, a thing of man. Unfortunately, the entire system of man operates from this faulty perspective.

God's perspective is this — He sees every detail of life and delights in all of it. Far beyond his delight in created life, is His love and honor of the Son. His word talks about Jesus!

> He was supreme in the beginning and — leading the resurrection parade — he is supreme in the end. From beginning to end he's there, towering far above everything, everyone. So spacious is he, so roomy, that everything of God finds its proper place in him without crowding. Not only that, but all the broken and dislocated pieces of the universe — people and things, animals and atoms — get properly fixed and fit together in vibrant harmonies, all because of his death, his blood that poured down from the Cross. 9

As a Life-giver we must learn to see from God's perspective. Jesus is the centerpiece of God's plan. Our model is Jesus, not one another.

Vision Without Understanding
Without discernment it is impossible to interpret what we see. Information is useless unless wisdom and understanding are present. I have seen enormous errors made in discernment and as a result whole groups of people have veered off into deception. It is impossible to explain adequately in this chapter all the ramifications of good guidance. I would recommend Bob Mumford's, *Take Another Look at Guidance* * for further study.

Here are a some very important things to keep in mind when trying to discern what we hear and see as guidance from the Lord. When you receive a promise from God do not jump to magical fantasies.

You might hear God say, "I am going to bless you." At first the meaning seems apparent. Bless means...A fine house, new cars, a prosperous profession. However, no material wealth is forth-coming. The imagined expectancy led to error. In reality God's blessing includes character development and the loss of all things for the sake of the Kingdom.

The route to the future unfolds gradually.

Mt. Hood is some one hundred miles to the east of here. On clear days it can appear to sit in the backyard. It looks so close, yet is so far away, miles and miles away. There is a city, two or three major rivers, canyons, hills, forests, snow, a gain of eight thousand feet in elevation, much danger, many miles. The traverse is long and difficult. Similarly, the process and cost to reach a spiritual goal may seem simple at first. However, God's way is not a straight line. The traverse of the journey is not completely apparent.

Recognize that any plan of God is usually given in seedform.

We get a grand idea, revelation, thought, a plan. We boldly declare, "It is from God!" God then says, "Let go of it, put it into the ground. Let it die." This seems paradoxical. God gives the idea and vision, then demands its death. We do not know that God has a great way to bring about His plan, not ours. At first we resist and do not give up the idea. Then the idea gradually dies. Faith in the plan fails. The whole thing is forgotten. Life continues. God however has not forgotten. The plan unfolds but is not recognized because the growing sprout is different from the seed, the plan. Years later His plan produces marvelous fruit. It is then that we remember the grand idea we had so long ago. God has completed the work. Now what was an idea has become reality. The fulfillment of that initial vision is far greater than what we could even imagine.

The word of God must be discerned correctly.

"Thanks Lord for that scripture. It applies perfectly to my circumstances." The personal application of a single passage can result in great insight and guidance or great error. The scriptures are to be "a lamp to our feet." However, so often scripture is applied with-

48

out wisdom. Scripture must not be taken out of historical context, out of textual context, out of language context. For us to see with comprehension, the word of God must be correctly understood as it is written and applied. It must not be treated as a magical incantation that puts God into an obligatory position to fulfill His word. The word is written to bring a clear witness of God's actions and God's intent. Read complete passages; know the context of the writings. Find the meaning of the original language. There is no excuse for irresponsible foolishness concerning the Word of God. Read the Word with comprehension.

It is difficult to interpret circumstances as they occur.

Often circumstances are misread because we rush to explain the event. In time God may tell you the reason; at other times He does not explain. Sometimes the full understanding of a season of life only comes with time. Be assured however, God tenderly watches over you.

The Lord's timing is not the same as ours.

God is more interested in the process and relationship, than the actual goal. He does not hurry through anything. He starts with the hidden things, the deep roots within, and works in His time frame to bring everything to completion. At this point in my life, I'm convinced that we never know how long He will take. We cry, "Why does healing take so long?" A lifetime seems an eternity to us. It is nothing to God.

Be assured spiritual blindness gradually lifts. We then say, "Ah, yes, now I see...Oh, there is more! And still *more,* Lord?" And yes, always *more.* He is faithful to reveal to us the Things of God." Oh, Yes...!

"Blessed are the pure in heart, for they shall see God." (Mt.5:8)

PRE –
OCCUPATION

*"And He began to teach them that the Son of Man must suffer
many things, and be rejected by the elders and scribes, and be
killed, and after three days rise again. He spoke this word openly. Then Peter took Him aside and began to rebuke Him. But
when He had turned around and looked at His disciples, He
rebuked Peter, saying, 'Get behind Me, Satan! for you are not
mindful of the things of God, but of the things of man.'"*
(Mk. 8:29,31-32)

Peter, characteristic of us all, was occupied with ordinary things,
the Things of Man, the kingdom of the 'i am.' Why do we act in
certain predictable ways? Why do we do the things we do? What
is it we are trying to achieve?

All of us have very definite emotional needs which we try to satisfy. Both children and adults need security, recognition, love
(belonging), and adventure.* We act in certain ways to obtain
emotional well-being. Age does not matter. Infants, as well as children, demand and find ways for these needs to be met. Adults are
motivated in similar ways. The inner motives can be clearly
observed in our interaction with each other.

We Need To Be Safe

Fear motivated Peter's screams of, "No, No! Jesus you are wrong. You won't suffer and die. No, it cannot happen!" Peter felt endangered by Jesus' words. Jesus' destiny did not make sense to Peter who knew the things of man, not the things of God. Peter could not believe the words that Jesus spoke, and as a consequence, rebuked the Lord. Fear led Peter to misstep. Do not be too hard on Peter. We too have a hard time trusting God to keep us safe and secure.

Our need for security starts at birth. However, some children are more fearful than others. If you watch children at play, it is easy to spot the fearful child. He will seldom break the rules. He takes few risks, says only the right things at the right time. He hangs back and does not climb the monkey bars. He doesn't shout and push. Mother is 'home base.' He is acutely aware of danger and avoids it. Sounds a bit familar, doesn't it.

Adults also seek security. Thoughts sound like this: *"If I can just say the right thing... I wonder what he wants me to do? Not me! No sir, I'm not sticking out my neck. If I do better than anyone expects, no one can criticize me..."* Comfort and safety are primary. People are unpredictable and therefore cause fear.

Fear is automatic and normal in an endangering situation. We run or fight. However, if ordinary life is perceived as dangerous, then a constant state of fear prevails and overwhelms reason. A person builds a system, a kingdom, a fortress, for protection from imagined danger. This causes separation from others behind walls of our own making. However, a fearful person is very needy and will use people for protection. A fearful woman will seek out a strong in-charge controlling man. The assertive man is used to make the plans, talk to others, take the initiative with the children. The woman can criticize from the side-lines without risking mistakes. A fearful man will marry a cheerful, self-reliant independent woman. This woman is left to run the house, plan the finances, and often earn the living. The fearful man can hide in silence and passivity.

This can lead to dependent relationships that cause conflict. Disappointment occurs and fear increases when another is used for security. A kingdom run by man is present when security and fear are the main preoccupation.

51

God does not want this to continue. He will reveal those hidden places deep within that allow a root of fear. It is imperative to recognize this preoccupation, seek God for the cause, and then watch as He enters the fortress of fear and begins a life-time assault upon the prison. Turn from the fear and seek deliverance and healing from the Lord.

We Need To Be Important — Preeminent — Recognized

Everyone wants to be recognized. Children want to know how they compare with the others. *"I'm the strongest." "No, I am!" "My daddy can beat yours up." "I can run faster than you." "You are ugly." "Well, you are stupid." "You can't catch me." "I'm in the red group, we're smart, we can read."* Contest is the name of the game. Within the group are those who seem superior and those who hope they are. Strangely enough, most feel inferior. No matter how competitive or passive, everyone needs to be seen and affirmed.

The need for recognition is often the driving force behind achievement. It seems essential to be the 'best,' the most important, the one who always does a good job, the richest and best dressed, the nicest, most friendly, the perfect follower of Christ. Life is a contest to see who is sufficiently different from the others in order to receive honor and recognition. Within the family one son will be the football star, another will excel in school. Another child will drop out, look weird, rebel, all for attention. Often this competitive spirit leads to rejection because others are also striving to be recognized. Everyone ends up stepping on everyone else in order to be seen. This occurs everywhere: politics, business, families, school, professions, churches.

The vie for attention is carried over to the Lord. Often we expect to be rejected from the Lord also. We feel outside the loop and invisible. It is so hard for us to realize that God always sees and knows us.

Jesus chose Peter for a destiny of greatness. He took him away from his trade and called him to become one of the most prominent and famous men in history. Jesus blessed him saying,

> Simon Bar-Jonah, flesh and blood has not revealed this to you, but My Father who is in heaven, And I also say to you that you are Peter, and on this rock I will build My

church, and the gates of Hades shall not prevail against it. And I will give you the keys of the kingdom of heaven, and whatever you bind on earth will be bound in heaven, and whatever you loose on earth will be loosed in heaven. (Mt.16: 17-19)

Peter could not conceive of God's plan and his part in it. Recognition came differently to Peter than he expected. He was given wisdom and power to reproduce all the miracles of Jesus. He was the head of a baby church. He was also destined to suffer and die for the Lord. Peter gained recognition and approval by being all that God had ordained for him to be.

You too will gain approval and recognition when committed to the Lord. Do not jump to any fantasy of fame and fortune. The goal of all of life is to come to know the Lord and be like Him. He waits for us to stop our preoccupation with achievement, attention, and uniqueness. When we turn to Him and see Him, everything else pales in comparison. To know yourself, you must know God. We then are free from the struggle for preeminence.

Paul states: I have learned in whatever state I am, to be content: I know how to be abased, and I know how to abound. Everywhere and in all things I have learned both to be full and to be hungry, both to abound and to suffer need. (Phil.4:11-12)

We Need To Be Loved
Everyone needs to be loved. Watch the children at play and catch a glimpse of yourself. The children are in groups. Some play handball; others enjoy foursquare. Some gather to visit. Still others join the crowd who plays soccer or the gang who parades up and down the school yard. The clique excludes the shy and clumsy boy, the socially inappropriate girl. Belonging to the group is of primary importance. The activity provides the cohesiveness of relationship; the group provides a place of belonging. Behavior is motivated by the need to belong, to be with others.

Much time and effort is spent trying to find love. We were created to belong to one another. (God knew that Adam needed a counterpart.) Most of us love to be loved. We also love to love. It is the natural thing to do. However relationships can become the center of our thoughts and the motivation of most of our activities.

The self is preoccupied, *"This sure is an unfriendly place. No one cares if I am here or not." "All I want is to be accepted." "The tavern guys are my friends. We enjoy just drinking together." "Can't we stay here and become involved with the community?" "Joe never understood me at all, neither did John, but you seem to care." "Please won't someone talk to me."*

It is not wrong to love or be loved. The difficulty occurs when love is a demand. "If you don't love me, you'll be sorry." "I love you so much, why do you act that way." "It is your fault that I'm like this. Change or I leave." "You are not the woman/man I married. You have lost your charm. I've found the perfect person to love me." Love has been cheapened and perverted. Some of us do not know how to love or how to receive love. Driven by this need, many go from one abortive relationship into another with disastrous results. Hopefully the coming chapters of this book will guide all of us into real and perfect love. Until we experience the love that comes from the Lord, we have hardly been cherished at all. His Love is the only love that satisfies.

Jesus loved Peter. In return, Peter loved Jesus. To think of his friend as dead was intolerable. Jesus spoke of his death, and in so doing, spoke of His love. God loves, and within love there is always suffering for the object of love. "Greater love has no one than this, than to lay down one's life for his friends." (Jn.15:13) A lover bears all pain, will endure incredible suffering to save the one whom he loves. Jesus intended to save all. This is God's way to show love. We are enamored with Him when we touch this eternal, passionate, sacrificial Love. We in turn, show God's love by sacrifice, giving life, taking the humble place, risking to love the afflicted.

We Need Adventure
Some children thrive on adventure. They love the risky edge, whether it be cliff or sport. Imagined danger and conquest fill each moment. They climb anything, dive off heights and sled down mountains. They love to read about the adventuresome who have conquered the world. They don't care about who is the greatest; they don't want to be safe, that is boring; they often cannot conform to a group. However, they organize others and lead them into bigger escapades.

Perhaps you relate to these children. Adventure of some sort is necessary for emotional health. If we look at how much time and money are invested in entertainment or sport, we then can gauge its importance. Passive adventure abounds. The mini wars of sports substitute for real battles. A wild tale of hide and seek keeps us glued to the television. The secret life of a double agent holds us spell bound. Others are not satisfied with passive participation. They love to rappel down mountains, wind surf, raft on white water, drive very fast, or sky dive. There are those who are challenged by the creation of new products, the resolution of difficult social situations, a new career. Ah, yes, adventure is necessary.

Peter's life turned upside down when he was with Jesus. Gone were the quiet days of fishing. Just to be with Jesus was exciting. One minute Jesus provoked the Pharisees with His wisdom, next, He performed miracles. The leprous ventured out of isolation for healing. The violent demon-possessed screamed for mercy. A fierce storm at sea frightened the disciples. Peter risked life and limb to walk on water. Who would think that he, Peter, would walk on water? Risk-taking was contagious. Peter loved this new life.

Boredom results when life narrows into routine and prescribed roles. For those who thrive on adventure, this sense of monotony is very painful. The challenge of change, discovery, new relationships, and creative ideas fuel the internal fires of the adventuresome.

Some are addicted to adventure. This, of course, is not healthy. To live for the next thrill, the next escape from the law, the next sporting event is extremely distracting. This preoccupation leads to increasing restlessness. Nothing quite satisfies the craving. More and more excitement seems to be needed, and yet nothing helps. Teens often express, "I'm bored." They want to be entertained, stimulated by excitement. No matter how much is spent on entertainment, video-games, 'fast' cars, sports, the lust will not go away. God alone can satisfy the need for adventure. We cannot imagine nor create adventure like the one Jesus gave Peter.

Dear Reader, adventure is part of the provision of God. His plan for you and me is beyond our greatest imagined thrill. My life as a believer has turned unexpected corners, led down paths of

incredible wonder far beyond my wildest dreams.
Great people, gentle saints, strong faithful believers have been
miraculously placed in my life. In fact, one of my worst habits is
to complain to the Lord about a new turn of events. He continually has to remind me, "Fret not. This is part of my plan for you."
Remember, seldom can we anticipate how He will meet this need
for adventure. Put aside the things of man and your anxiously laid
plans. The Lord is leading out into adventure and conquests. He
invites us to join Him. He commands, "Follow Me!"

God Knows Our Need

God alone can meet the inner need for love, security, recognition,
and adventure. The Father was the source of everthing that Jesus
needed. God meets our need; people are to be enjoyed and loved.
Jesus did not satisfy his need through people. Therefore they were
able to come to Him in complete freedom. He loved them, but did
not need them. We strive to obtain and possess safety, approval,
intimacy and excitement because we do not believe that God will
provide everything to guarantee emotional health. God will not
compete for control. He stands aside and lets us try. We find ourselves afraid much of the time since our schemes and plans fail to
bring satisfaction. We are preoccupied with the effort. It is much
easier to let him have the honor. He will provide everything that
is needed for emotional health and well being.

> But what happens when we live God's way? He brings
> gifts into our lives, much the same way that fruit appears
> in an orchard — things like affection for others, exuber-
> ance about life, serentiy. We develop a willingness to stick
> with things, a sense of compassion in the heart, and a con-
> viction that a basic holiness permeates things and people.
> We find ourselves involved in loyal commitments, not
> needing to force our way in life, able to marshal and
> direct our energies wisely. (Gal.5:22-23) 1

NOTES:

Section 2
Things Of Man

Chapter 3
Things Of Man
1 Eugene Peterson, *The Message,* (Colorado Springs, Colorado: Navpress, 1993)p.209
"And Jesus said,"For judgment I have come into this world, that those who do not see may see, and that those who see may be made blind." (Jn.9:39 NKJ)
2 Peterson, *The Message,* p.151
"And He said to them,"Take heed and beware of covetousness, for one's life does not consist in the abundance of the things he possesses." Then He spoke a parable to them, saying:"The ground of a certain rich man yielded plentifully. And he thought within himself, saying,'What shall I do , since I have no room to store my crops?' "So he said,' I will do this: I will pull down my barns and build greater, and there I will store all my crops and my goods. And I will say to my soul,"Soul, you have many goods laid up for many years; take your ease; eat, drink, and be merry."' "But God said to him,'Fool!This night your soul will be required of you; then whose will those things be which you have provided?'"So is he who lays up treasure for himself, and is not rich toward God." (Lk.12:15-21 NKJ)
3 Peterson, *The Message,* p. 328.
"I beseech you therefore, brethren, by the mercies of God, that you present your bodies a living sacrifice, holy, acceptable to God, which is your reasonable service. And do not be conformed to this world, but be transformed by the renewing of your mind, that you may prove what is that good and acceptable and perfect will of God. For I say, through the grace given to me, to everyone who is among you, not to think of himself more highly than he ought to think, but to think soberly, as God has dealt to each one a measure of faith. (Rom.12:1-3 NKJ)

Chapter 4
Born Blind
1 Peterson, *The Message,* p.373
"But even if our gospel is veiled, it is veiled to those who are

perishing, whose minds the god of this age has blinded, who do not believe, lest the light of the gospel of the glory of Christ, who is the image of God, should shine on them." (II Cor.4:3-4 NKJ)

2 *Webster's New World Dictionary,*(Cleveland, New York, The World Publishing Co. 1956)p.1631

3 *Webster's New World Dictionary,*(Cleveland, New York, The World Publishing Co. 1956)p.1245

4 Peterson, *The Message,* p.305

"For the wrath of God is revealed from heaven against all ungodliness and unrighteousness of men, who suppress the truth in unrighteousness because what may be known of God is manifest in them, for God has shown it to them. For since the creation of the world His invisible attributes are clearly seen, being understood by the things that are made, even His eternal power and Godhead, so that they are without excuse, because, although they knew God they did not glorify Him as God, nor were thankful, but became futile in their thoughts, and their foolish hearts were darkened." (Rom. 1:18-21 NKJ)

5 Peterson, *The Message,* p 520.

"I know your works, that you are neither cold nor hot. I could wish you were cold or hot. So then, because you are lukewarm, and neither cold nor hot, I will vomit you out of My mouth. Because you say, 'I am rich, have become wealthy, and have need of nothing; — and do not know that you are wretched, miserable, poor, blind, and naked —"(Rev. 3:15-17 NKJ)

6 *Webster's New World Dictionary,*(Cleveland, New York, The World Publishing Co. 1956)p.484.

7 Peterson, *The Message,* p 520.

"I counsel you to buy from Me gold refined in the fire, that you may be rich; and white garments, that you may be clothed, that the shame of your nakedness may not be revealed; and anoint your eyes with eye salve, that you may see. As many as I love, I rebuke and chasten. Therefore be zealous and repent."
(Rev.3:18-19 NKJ)

8 *Webster's New World Dictionary,*(Cleveland, New York, The World Publishing Co. 1956) p.1092.

* DeVern Fromke, *Unto Full Stature* (Cloverdale, Ind., Ministry of Life, Inc. 1964) p. 106

9 Peterson, *The Message,* p422.

"And He is before all things, and in Him all things consist. And He is the head of the body, the church, who is the firstborn from the dead, that in all things He may have the preeminence.

or it pleased the Father that in Him all the fullness should dwell and by Him to reconcile all things to Himself, by Him, whether things on earth or things in heaven, having made peace through the blood of His cross." (Col.1:17-20 NKJ)
* Bod Mumford, *Take Another Look At Guidance*, (Raleigh, N.C., Lifechangers Publishing. 1993)

Chapter 5
Pre-occupation
* Bob Mumford,*Christ in Session*, (Bob Mumford)p.15.
1 Peterson, *The Message,* p.398.
"But the fruit of the Spirit is love, joy, peace, longsuffering, kindness, goodness, faithfulness, gentleness, self-control. Against such there is no law." (Gal.5:22-23 NKJ)

FOLLOW TO
ESTABLISH
FOUNDATION

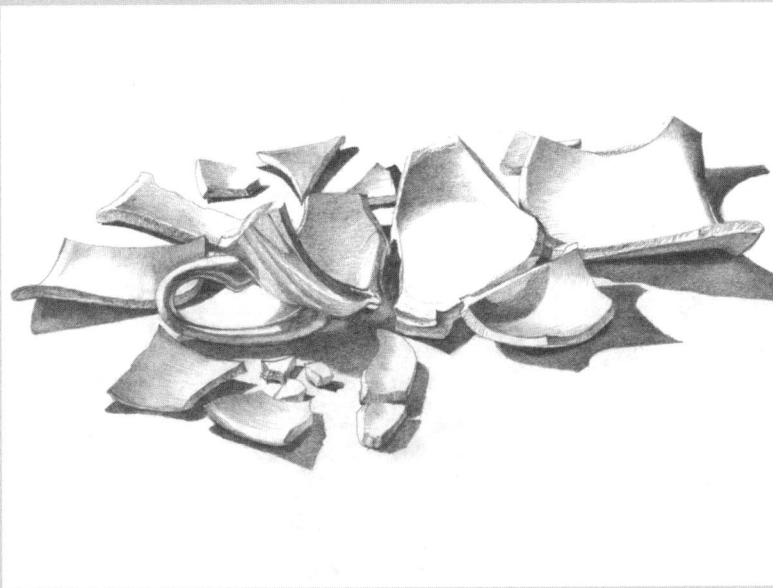

"Whoever desires to come after Me,

let him deny himself,

take up his cross,

follow Me!

(Mk.8:34)

c h a p t e r

6

IMAGE AND DESIRE

"Whoever desires to come after Me... (Mk.8:34)

Jesus passionately called to the people, "Whoever desires to come after Me let him deny himself, take up your cross, and follow Me." The next three chapters explain in detail this one sentence. This familiar scripture is extremely important to understand. What makes us desire to know and follow the Lord? What does deny yourself mean? What exactly is your cross? If we desire to follow Him, then we will experience life as He lived it. We have learned the theology behind "The Things of God" and "The Things of Man," now it is time to move into the messy life experience where God forcefully presses us into the image of His Son.

A child loves presents. He enthusiastically rips open the packages to investigate and play with each for a short time, then he moves on to the next. Natural man, like the child, focuses upon what he receives. Sadly, his (her) wants seldom match the Gift God gave. The Things of God and the Things of Man are antagonistic to each other.

God gave only one Present, His most extravagant and wondrous Gift. He gave Jesus. Within this Gift, all other things reside. The more we investigate the Gift, the more there is to find. The more we enjoy Him, the more delighted He is. This Gift neither wears out nor does He become obsolete or monotonous. The question is, will the Gift even be noticed? Will God's Present be desired, received and appreciated? How does anyone come to desire God? Where does desire originate?

The Image
God created man with an internal pattern, an image of Himself. We resemble God; we are not God. God is the perfect model, the ideal, the guide, and the standard. We are made in the image of God, (Gen.1:26) and therefore, have within a picture of God: his righteousness and holiness, his dominion and power. Therefore, we know intuitively good from evil, right from wrong, order from chaos, light from darkness. This imprint, the shadow of God's perfection and love, enables us to recognize God through the evidence of creation.

What may be known of God is manifest in them, for God has shown it to them. For since the creation of the world His invisible attributes are clearly seen, being understood by the things that are made, even His eternal power and Godhead, so that they are without excuse..." (Rom.1:19-20)

After Adam and Eve disobeyed God, they lost the privilege and joy of communion with Him. However, their longing to be with Him remained. It is this yearning that draws us towards Him.

We recognize God intuitively. For instance, we know something of God, the extraordinary value of new life, when we hold a new born baby. We know something of God, a power beyond human dimensions, when we marvel at the terrifying force of a mighty storm. We sense something of God, His creative genius, when we see the beautiful subtle colors of early morning light. We participate in a tiny piece of God and his love when we cry with a friend, dance for joy, shelter a little critter.

We know of His perfection and completeness in little flashes of revelation. I call these "sparkle encounters," for each one contains a tiny light-filled peek at God. These glimmers that happen over and over again lead us to hunger for God. Unbelievers usually do not recognize these as the way God reveals Himself. Yet, as these many small "sparkle" encounters are experienced, belief in God grows. This is pre-conversion; it is not conversion. I am convinced that this is how God the Spirit draws us to the Father and the Son. At some point, we believe enough to confess Jesus as Savior and Lord. The declaration of His existence, His life and death, His resurrection, is essential. However, this is just the beginning of the revelation of God.

Desire To Know Him

Throughout my entire life I have enjoyed these wonderful little "sparkle" encounters. Each has added to my desire to know Him more and more. Here are a few of these little encounters that drew me to Christ.

I remember at a very young age, sitting on a window sill watching the sunrise. I loved the soft gentleness of the dawn and the warmth of the early morning sun. The beauty and quietness of daybreak was a "sparkle" encounter.

Mother and I attended early morning communion service. Although there was neither music nor sermon I enjoyed the reverent simplicity of worship. I heard the truth of Jesus' death and resurrection. Even as a child I joined the adults and prayed:

> Almighty God, to you all hearts are open, all desires known, and from you no secrets are hid: Cleanse the thoughts of our hearts by the inspiration of your Holy Spirit, that we may perfectly love you, and worthily magnify your holy Name; through Christ our Lord. Amen. 1

The mystery of communion was a glimpse of His Presence.

Every Saturday I listened to the "Unshackled" program on the radio. Like the men and women in the stories, I too wanted to experience freedom from a life of sin. (I didn't know what sin was but I knew it must be was awful.) The promise of a changed life was a peek at salvation.

Motion pictures about Biblical times were very exciting to me. I wanted to experience the things that I saw in the movies. The dramatization of Jesus' life was a picture of the real Jesus.

When I was in my early twenties I met some people who seemed to know Jesus. As my host fixed dinner, she radiated a warmth and love which I knew was the Lord. I was very curious to know how anyone could be happy cooking dinner in one hundred degree heat. The meal included homemade lemon meringue pie. (Maybe that doesn't seem miraculous to you, but it was for me.) I asked questions. I heard about Jesus. His presence in their lives was revelation to me.

One night as I worked on an orthopedic ward at County Hospital, a disoriented lady screamed over and over again, "Help Me! Won't someone help me." I finally went into her room, shut the door, and tried an experiment. (I still was not sure about any of this God stuff.) However, I knew the Bible said we had authority to release healing to others. I tested this out; gently laying my hand on her, I said, "Peace, be still. The Lord is here. Don't be afraid." She stopped her thrashing about and went to sleep. I was shocked. This exciting experience increased my hunger to know the Lord.

Truth Encounters
The small spiritual encounters form a fabric of experiential belief. This matrix of belief grows in another way also. The image of God gives us the innate ability to 'hear' truth.

Even very young children have an uncanny sense of truth. Just try telling them a lie; they know something is wrong. They pick up unspoken messages within the family. They know when a mother is sick even if she acts well. They know when the parents are having a disagreement even when it is done behind closed doors.

Short pithy sayings also 'ring a bell' of rightness, of truth.
> A job worth doing is worth doing well.
> If you don't know the rules, you can't play the game.
> A bird in the hand is worth two in the bush.
> A penny saved is a penny earned.
> Make hay while the sun shines.
> You can lead a horse to water but you can't make it drink.
> You can't teach an old dog new tricks.
> A man's ways will find him out.
> If you clean the corners, the middle takes care of itself.
> Turn about is fair play.
> Don't stir the cow pies...it stinketh worse.
> An apple a day keeps the doctor away.

The list is endless. If you stop for a moment, I am certain that you also can add one or two sayings to the list. These sayings are true although not particularly biblical. They do contain folk wisdom, the little laws of life. They are glimpses of truth.

The Holy Spirit uses truth to draw us to God for we *know* when truth is spoken. As Billy Graham preaches, his words ring true, even to the unbeliever. Mother Teresea speaks with authority as she tells of her Jesus, her God. People listen because her life itself reveals truth. It matches their God image within.

Truth is taught by experience also. A parent can say, "Don't do this...Don't do that..." The child will often do that precise thing and find out 'the truth.' Researchers find truth as they experiment. These are endeavors in a search for truth. The more they discover, the more truth points to the Creator.

The Old Testament is a record of God's interaction with His people. It is written to provide an unchanging picture or pattern of God, the revelation of the unseen God. It is truth laid out in written form. The history of the Hebrews covered thousands of years. God's pursuit of them, and the lessons that He taught are recorded truth. The Old Testament is an unchanging guide to truth, ancient, preserved truth! The Old Testament has been preserved perfectly for thousands of years. No other piece of written material comes even close to the miracle of this document. Its preservation alone is a testimony to God's sovereign ordination of these writings.

When Jesus appeared upon the earth, He was Truth incarnate. He spoke with authority; He healed with power; He loved with tenderness; He manifested Life. An incomplete portrait of God was known; Jesus completed the picture.

These truth encounters woven with the "sparkle" encounters lead to increasing belief in God. This God-given ability to believe enables us to shed the Things of Man and desire the Things of God. This process is called transformation.

An analogy may help illustrate how the Things of God are apprehended and why the Things of Man become unimportant.

The image of God is imprinted within each of us. It is a gift.

God gave Jonathan, our son, an extraordinary love of sound. As a baby, he would notice and turn towards any unusual sound. Even as a little guy, he sang all the time with perfect pitch and tone. He listened to everything. The sound of his boot pulling out of mud, was a wonder to him. When he heard the bass viola played, he laid on the floor, put his ear to the ground to hear and feel the vibration. He was enthralled with the wondrous music of the "Nutcracker" ballet. A referee's whistle at a football game was replicated with his voice. God gave him this love of sound and the ability to hear 'music' everywhere.

In the same manner, God gives us his image and a desire to know Him. We respond automatically.

The transformation of a general image of God into a specific, organized, focused, and accurate picture of God is learned.

Ability and talent are God given. The translation of that talent into the performance of music is learned. Jon learned to play the piano and flute. Before he tried to play a piece of music on the piano, he first listened to a recording of a technically perfect performance of that composition. He became familiar with the piece as he listened to the recording over and over again. Before long, He could sing the melody and then harmony, and hear the piece within himself. He now had a perfect replica imprinted within, even though he could not perform the music.

We, so to speak, listen to truth and see the sparkle encounters. We note over and over again the presence of the Lord and the truth of His existence. Finally, belief becomes a part of us, just as the music became a part of Jonathan. This is how the Spirit of God builds our faith.

Later Jonathan studied the written music. He saw with his eyes the visual language that replicated the auditory language of the music. Hearing became seeing.

The word of God, like the written music, is an unchanging standard by which we measure our experience. It is written truth.

*The Image of God becomes the expressed Life of God as it flows
from the believer to others.*

Jonathan was not satisfied to only hear and see music. He wanted
to perform it. This required hours of practice. He learned the difficult runs and passages, the right hand and then, the left. During
practice the separate parts were unrelated to each other; the
beginning might be practiced last; the bridge into another theme,
played without either section. It sounded a mess. However, he
knew immediately when a note was wrong, for his internal standard of a technically perfect performance "spoke" to him. The
incorrect sound neither matched the internalized music nor the
written music. The auditory pattern learned from the tape did not
change; the written music remained the same. His performance
had to replicate the written and performed sound. Finally after
much work, the music, whether a simple tune like "Mary Had a Little Lamb" or a Sonata or Fugue, emerged without mistake.

*If we desire to go beyond the initial imprinting of belief in God,
we must do precisely the same as Jonathan. Our seeing of God
and our hearing of truth must be practiced. It is imperative to
diligently seek Him. There is great reward!*

> Without faith it is impossible to please Him, for he who
> comes to God must believe that He is, and that He is the
> rewarder of those who diligently seek Him. (Heb. 11:6)

Love for Jesus motivates us to seek Him.

Jonathan loved music which motivated his practice.

*As we see God we love Him more. This increases the desire to
apprehend Him. We are better able to discern His Presence as
we grow more acquainted with the written word. As faith
becomes practice we no longer just copy Him. We become an
expression of His Life.*

To continue our analogy — Jonathan's mastery of the composition
was not complete even if the piece was played correctly. A computer can perform technically correct music, without personality,
without life. As the complicated passages became easy, Jon added
expression and beauty. He enjoyed his own interpretations. Just

68

for fun he would play the piece "blue." It sounded deep, cold, sad and absolutely clear, crystalline. With a twinkle in his eye and a grin, he then played it "orange." If sound could have color, the mood of the music varied from a hot fiery red, to yellow, to orange, literally burning with passion and heat. His teacher strongly objected when "orange" revved up a Bach prelude. (Bach would object also.) One of his favorite pastimes was to play a Bach invention with a jazz syncopation. What fun! The music expressed his own unique inner 'song.' No one could play it quite as he did. Eventually he could play without written music. His gift was often shared for the enjoyment and delight of others.

As he matured in ability and understanding of music, he created his own compositions, more perfectly expressing his own unique "music language." The ever increasing knowledge base and performance expertise had no limitations. He loved sound; he loved music; he loved expressing himself in this language form. Jonathan continues today to listen to everything, to write music, to sing, to play flute and keyboard. Music is his favorite media for worship of the Lord who gave him this gift.

When the inner image of God, the Truth of God, and Jesus become ours, we express Life, His Life. We love God; we love His Presence; we love to express His Life, the language of a Life-giver.

> Beloved, now we are children of God; and it has not yet been revealed what we shall be, but we know that when He is revealed, we shall be like Him, for we shall see Him as He is. And everyone who has this hope in Him purifies himself, just as He is pure. (1 Jn.3:2-3)

DENY YOURSELF

"Whoever desires to come after Me, let him deny himself..."

Jesus challenged the crowd: "Do you want to follow me? It will cost. If you take the challenge, your life will change. Deny yourself, and take up your cross!" If you had been in the crowd what would you have asked? Do I have to leave my family and friends? Do I have to change my occupation? How soon do I leave? What does He mean?

Jesus showed the way as He denied himself. The Apostle Paul in the epistle to the Philippians outlines the way.

> Let this mind be in you which was also in Christ Jesus, who, being in the form of God, did not consider it robbery to be equal with God, *but made Himself of no reputation, taking the form of a bondservant,* and *coming in the likeness of men.* And being found in appearance as a man, *He humbled Himself and became obedient* to the point of death, even the death of the cross. (Phil. 2:7-8)

The Word (Jesus) Was With God
Being in the form of God, did not consider it robbery to be equal with God
Jesus, equal with God, with no beginning and unlimited in power, is the Fountainhead of all Life. The Apostle John describes the Fountainhead.

In the beginning was the Word, and the Word was with God, and the Word was God. He was in the beginning with God. All things were made through Him, and without Him nothing was made that was made. In Him was life, and the life was the light of men. (Jn.1:1-4)

The prophet Daniel describes the Lord of Glory.

I lifted up my eyes and looked, and behold, a certain man clothed in linen, whose waist was girded with gold of Uphaz! His body was like beryl, his face like the appearance of lightning, his eyes like torches of fire, his arms and feet like burnished bronze in color, and the sound of his words like the voice of a multitude...(Dan.10:5-6)

Jesus Begins The Great Assignment Of Lifegiver
I wonder how Jesus began the Assignment. Did He discuss with others what it would be like? Did He study for a test? Paul gives us a glimpse into the heavenly realm. History records His arrival. The rest is left to imagination. This is how it might have been.

Jesus made Himself of no reputation...
Jesus the King of Kings and Lord of Lords rises and kneels before the Father.
Jesus gives to the Father His Sovereignty and Dominion.*
His scepter is surrendered —
      He is now without dominion.
His sword is laid down —
      He is now without protection.
His crown is removed —
      His head is now bare.
His robe is removed —
      His body is now uncovered.
His shoes are removed —
      His feet are now exposed.
The outward symbols of kingly reputation are in the Father's hands.
The Son is enveloped in magnificent, splendorous light.

He leaves his Glory —
      honor
      power

riches
beauty
worship
splendor
He bows before the Father —
The Father loves the Son!

Jesus takes the form of a bondservant...
Jesus says: "Father, I am your slave. (servant)
         Not out of debt, but out of love.

Jesus starts His assignment as Lifegiver with nothing. We are to do
the same.

* * *

Our Mission Begins
Deny yourself!
"How can I get what I want when I want it?" is the cry of natural
man. A little baby is wonderful; he also rules his small kingdom.
He makes his needs known. If neglected, he screams. If uncomfortable, he screams. If hungry, he screams. He is only a baby; this
is normal. Unfortunately many do not shed this behavior as they
grow older. Jesus demands, "if you want to come after me, leave
the childishness and deny yourself..." (author's paraphrase) Our
trappings of self-aggrandizement, self-protection and self-centeredness must be left behind.

Our kingdoms manifest in many ways. A very practical vignette
might help you to recognize these inner kingdoms. Come with
me into the kitchen. Notice the garbage in the corner that needs
to be taken out. By common agreement, this is the husband's job.
He has not done it.

The wife sweetly asks, "Honey, would you please take the garbage
out?" These are her spoken words, but she has unspoken
thoughts, thoughts of her rights, her kingdom where she is judge.
*"Why do I always have to remind him about the garbage? We
have been married ten years, and he still needs reminding. He
is worse than the kids. I wonder how much accumulated
garbage it would take for him to even notice? I have enough to
do minding the kids without adding him to my duties."*

72

Nothing more is said.

The husband has his own kingdom. He heard the request and gives an assenting grunt. He, too, has his inner thoughts of his 'i am' kingdom. *"Always nagging. Every week the same thing. I've worked all day. I just want to watch the news and rest, but no, do this, do that. I feel like a slave. The only reason they think I'm here is to bring home the money for them to spend. Can't even have a little peace in my own home."*

Dinner is served. The wife bangs the plates on the table and glowers in hubby's direction. "Dinner's ready, please come!" He sits several minutes before slowly rising from his chair. He says nothing as he eats the meal. The garbage is still in the kitchen. The wife is furious at his irresponsibility. The husband is resistive and withdrawn.

Sound familiar? I hope not. Unfortunately, this little inner scene, and its variants, is very common. Our little kingdoms —

There is another way to live — it is to give up the kingdoms.

God created man to order, name and be in control, to have dominion over all created life. God was to help Adam rule. Adam and Eve thought they could rule without God. God let them try. Satan promised man dominion; death was the result. The first family produced the murderer Cain. Like Adam we need the Sovereign One to instruct us. To rule without help from the Lord is hard work, an never ending battle between "what you want," and "what I want." Conflict inevitably breaks out. Have you ever wondered where war comes from?

> Where do you think all these appalling wars and quarrels come from? Do you think they just happen? Think again. They come about because you want your own way, and fight for it deep inside yourselves. You lust for what you don't have and are willing to kill to get it. You want what isn't yours and will risk violence to get your hands on it. 1

If we do not allow God to be in charge, we strive to maintain "our" rights. Unfortunately this is not how it should be. God demands preeminence.

73

The Kingdom of God has one great King. He will not share His preeminence.

This seems obvious, yet it is difficult to acknowledge the rulership of God. We want to run our own lives with all of our energy and effort. For us to follow the Lord, we must yield to Him and give him control.

I gave a mini sermon on the Kingdom of God to a group of children. I asked them to describe a kingdom. They told of knights and castles. They knew that a kingdom usually had a king or a queen. I then explained that God's Kingdom had one King. A little five year old girl raised her hand and asked, "Can I be the king!" "No, you cannot be king because Jesus is the King," I answered. We went on with the lesson. Again she raised her hand, "I want to be the king!" "No you can't, you may be a princess. Would you like that? She remained unimpressed. She raised her hand again and assertively suggested, "Let's play presidents!"

My little friend stated a common reality of life. The King, a sovereign ruler, is not wanted. Who wants a King when we can have a president? Indeed, if all goes well, one day we might become the President of our little domain. It is hoped that by cultivating friendships with the rich and famous, accumulating a lot of money, and using power, it might be possible.

Returning to reality and in all seriousness, if you are to follow Jesus, choices must be made. Jesus cries, "Deny yourself!" Sometimes you might say, "Have it all! Take my great accomplishments, future plans, wealth, reputation." At other times, it is more difficult. You cry, "Not my job!" "Not my house!" "Not my children!" "Not my ministry!" "Not my reputation!" "Not my ideas!" "Not my plans!" "Not my time!" It is sometimes difficult to yield all to the Lord.

Let's go back to the kitchen and the war over the garbage. This is an example of how to yield to the Lord. The wife stops and listens to her inner self. *"I am so angry. What was it Lord that caused me to become so angry?"* His quiet voice speaks into her spirit, *"It is because you feel alone. You need someone to help but no one is there for you. I know your pain. I am here. Listen carefully — I care."*

The husband sits in his chair and feels miserable. *"Why don't I take the garbage out?"* The inner voice of the Spirit answers, *"You want to have a life of ease. You don't like serving the family. I know you need to be cared for. Let me show you the reward of a servant."* He says out loud, "Honey, I'm sorry you had to ask me again to take out the garbage. Please pray that I'll be more thoughtful. I'll do it right now. And by the way, this is a great dinner. Thanks!"

All have needs. We want someone else to meet our demands. The Lord nudges and asks, "Who is in control? Can any of your needs be met by demand? Yield. You are not preeminent, I AM."

The yielding of my childish demands occurs in tiny little increments throughout each day. God can help me if I let Him. He is within and will cause me to feel guilty when I take advantage of others to get my way. This guilty feeling gets my attention. I then can either ignore it and go on with my "need campaign", or I can ask Him what has caused the problem. He gently reminds me to place my demands before Him. He can bring me all that I need in very ingenious ways.

We must deliberately lay aside the *weapons of preeminence*. The *scepter* of our kingdom is the big stick of threats, manipulation, and coercion. "If you don't do this I'll..." The *sword* is cutting words and hurtful mean thoughts. "You stupid idiot, you will never learn." The *crown* is pride that does not allow us to admit: we are wrong, we don't know it all, we have been insensitive to others. The *robe* is the covering of self-righteousness that protects the weak, afraid, sinful person within. The *shoes* are the lies said to cover our tracks: the defensiveness, the reasonings, the excuses. The threats, cutting words, pride, self-righteousness and lies must be confessed to the Lord and to those we hurt. This behavior of a little dictator must be discarded. Then we become vulnerable, teachable, repentant. *Vulnerability* allows us to be tender to the Lord and to others. He always speaks with a voice of mercy and grace, truth and righteousness, love and security. *Teachability* allows us to learn the wisdom of God. He is able to give us knowledge beyond our limited resources. *Repentance* turns us towards God. It opens the way for our ways to change. This is His way.

An Example — Deny Yourself

This is a testimony of a man who left behind his kingdom that he had defended with harmful attitudes and behavior. This man ruled his life with rage, hatred, fantasy and despair. He lived a life of death, if that is possible. This is a story of God's redemption, the buying back of a life that was ruined. Do not let the extremes of this example distract you, for we are all enmeshed in self-protection, self-centeredness, and self-rejection.

When I first met this man he seemed to be mentally slow; his smile reserved. "Why have you come to see me?" I asked. He was not sure. "I don't know exactly. Someone thought it might help." Slumped in his chair he mumbled, "I feel terrible. I hate my life and want to die. I've tried to change, it's no use!"

As we became acquainted, he disclosed horrendous childhood abuse in which he had been repeatedly sodomized by his father. He exploded in rage, "I'm so mad at my father. He died before I told him how much I hate him! I Hate Him! I HATE HIM! He Killed Mom!" The terror of life behind the doors of "home", included the neglect of his mother during an illness which resulted in her death. My friend was only ten when his mother died. She was his only safe person, and then she was gone.

The abuse of this young boy now began in earnest. His father sold him to a man who ran a child prostitution ring. At the age of fourteen he ran away. He stole cars, was arrested, and returned to his father who continued to abuse him. He ran away again. He used drugs and alcohol, stole anything he wanted and slept anyplace he could. Survival was his life. Eventually he found a good job, married, had children, and in turn, abused them. He had vowed, "I will never, never be like my father!" He was just like him. He now understood what drove his father.

He raged about his abuse. He raged against himself. He was like a boiling cauldron filled with rage. He raged against God, "It's your fault! You could have stopped it. You don't care!" One night he read about Jesus...cursed, beaten, condemned, hated, falsely accused, tortured...He wondered if God might understand his anger and hatred after-all.

His Healing
He Left Rage Behind
To give the Lord his anger and rage was not accomplished with a cheap and meaningless, "I forgive you." Week after week he raged until his spirit finally let go of all the hatred he had carried since childhood.

Releasing his mother to the Lord was very difficult. During one of our times together, he used a memory to help actualize his mother's death so he could say good-bye. He remembered mother on a path in a forest. She appeared as if near death, very weak, thin and sick. He saw himself as a little boy holding his Mom's hand. They walked slowly down this lonely path through the trees. He stopped and said "Good-bye, Mama." He then wept uncontrollably for a long time. Finally the childhood agony dissipated and the sobbing stopped. Then...He 'saw' her continue on down the path without him. She was no longer old and sick, she had turned into a beautiful young woman who stopped to pick wild flowers and to continue along the path until he could see her no longer. He knew Jesus had graced this good-bye and understood his agony. Life changed. His rage stopped; he chose to forgive his evil parent.

He Left Fantasy Behind
The feeling of helplessness was ever present due to his victimization. To relieve his despair, He made up stories about wonderful people and places. Real life interrupted the fantasy. Finally he had the courage to stop escaping into an imagined world.

He Left A Distorted Self-image Behind
He discovered that the worthless, hopeless feelings about himself were based upon what his father had told him, and were untrue. He had always believed he was stupid

77

and unable to achieve. Instead, he discovered that he could think, plan, and create. He went back to school, started at third grade level and continued through grade school, high school, and eventually graduated from college.

He Left Mistrust Behind
He was suspicious and mistrusting. He had survived the abuse, the terrible years all alone; it was safer that way. His wife and kids hated him. He begged for forgiveness. He wept bitter tears. He finally forgave himself, and slowly his family grew to trust him.

This is a true story. However, I have changed some identifying facts to protect confidentiality. The Lord brought down the kingdom of this courageous friend. He let go of everything he had erroneously come to believe to apprehend the Kingdom of God.

* * *

Your story might not include abuse or these particulars. However, the old life in our kingdom has many of the same symptoms: hatred, anger, rage, grief, fantasy, distorted self-image, dull mind, idle dreams, fear and mistrust.

Giving up man's kingdom is only preparatory —

Take The Form Of A Bondslave
To give up my little kingdom is one thing, to become a slave is quite another. A bondslave willingly chose to be a slave because he loved and trusted his master. He had no rights of his own. In the same manner, *to give Jesus control of my life is the issue.* Life is no longer about what I want, what I think, what I need, what I know, what I achieve. It is about what God wants, thinks, needs, knows, and achieves. Can you see the difference? At first, Paul's life was about Paul. After Paul talked to Jesus on the road to Damascus, his life was about Jesus. Likewise, Jesus' life was about the Father. He revealed the Father. He did what the Father did. He spoke words sent by the Father. His wisdom came from the Father. His death was the Father's will.

This is radical in its implications. How to be a bondslave of the Lord is learned over a whole life time. The commitment comes first, then the course ahead unfolds. This is the departure point for those who hunger and desire to come after the Lord. The apostle Paul expresses his passion for the Lord in his letter to the Philippians. This passionate scripture gives a glimpse of the future for those who follow the Lord.

> Yet indeed I also count all things loss for the excellence of the knowledge of Christ Jesus my Lord, for whom I have suffered the loss of all things, and count them as rubbish, that I may gain Christ and be found in Him, not having my own righteousness, which is from the law, but that which is through faith in Christ, the righteousness which is from God by faith; that I may know Him and the power of His resurrection, and the fellowship of His sufferings, being conformed to His death, if, by any means, I may attain to the resurrection from the dead. Not that I have already attained, or am already perfected; but I press on, that I may lay hold of that for which Christ Jesus has also laid hold of me. Brethren, I do not count myself to have apprehended; but one thing I do, forgetting those things which are behind and reaching forward to those things which are ahead, I press toward the goal for the prize of the upward call of God in Christ Jesus. (Phil. 3:8-14)

Y O U R
C R O S S

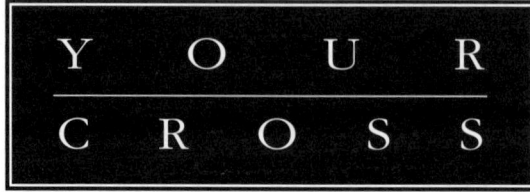

"...take up your cross and follow Me!"

Now pick up your cross and let's get on with the mission. What is the cross? What do we take along as we follow Jesus? When I helped my Dad, he would turn to me and say, "Get the Phillips screwdriver." I had no idea what he wanted, yet I was too proud, too afraid, to ask. I brought him my best guess. Impatiently he waved it away saying, "No, no, the Phillips screwdriver!" Do you know what the cross really is, or do you just hope your guess is accurate?

The Cross
The cross we carry is not a thing. The cross is our ordinary human life, the unique person God has made us to be: the gene pattern, physical appearance, intelligence, personality type, emotive style, talents, weaknesses, time of birth, location, and family. *You and I are to follow the Lord.* Our humanity is the cross. Many do not love themselves as God made them. They covet the gifts and talents of others, assuming that such gifts make them worthy to follow the Lord. They say, "It would be great to be talented, good looking, intelligent, coordinated, rich, and extroverted. At least, it would be nice to be 'normal.'" Their ethnic origin, financial situation, and upbringing seem less fortunate than that of others. Stereotypical ideals and fanciful traits are desired. This discontentment often erupts into anger or despair. "Why am I like this! Can't I get rid of me?" No, *you* are to follow the Lord.

God's Love The Foundation Of Life

God loves *you*. If God held you as a newborn in His hand, He might say, "Little child, I formed you in your mother's womb; I know you intimately; I watch over you day and night; I call you by name; I love you; I have redeemed you; I have your days written in my book." The scriptures declare God's love for each individual over and over again. He loved us before we were born, before we could have known Him. A baby is naked, needy, dependent, and yet loved by God. An infant owns nothing, thinks no profound thoughts, performs no great feats, and still the infant is loved. The value of just one little life is beyond measure. The newborn baby held in His hand is valuable, wondrous, filled with life. God loves this baby, this child.

His love is the foundation of life.* When you realize how secure you are in His love, you will not be afraid. The Lord says, "I love you, just the way you are. You are welcome to follow me. Come, as we walk together I will transform you so that you can love as I love. You have become very confused about who you are, and what you have been created to be. You are broken; you are defensive. You show me your accomplishments instead of revealing who you are. You are consumed with yourself. You resist my invitation. I know this. Come anyway. Come, follow me!"

* * *

On my bookcase, a broken white coffee cup sits in a heap of small and large pieces. Most who see the cup eventually ask, "I suppose that broken cup has a meaning?" "Yes," I say, "the cup represents you. Would you like to know why it is here?"

I use it to explain transformation. I place the pieces of the cup in a pile on my desk. I then pick up the largest piece, the side of the cup. "This looks like a whole cup from this side. You might be like this cup; it is easy to appear whole when in fact, you are broken. This kind of pretense is excruciatingly painful because people demand, "Act right!" They cannot hear your silent desperate cry, *"Doesn't anyone notice? I have nothing to give. I'm broken"*

The next piece I show is the handle. By this time my counselee has caught on, "Oh, I wouldn't show that piece, someone might get a handle on me."

I pick up the bottom of the cup. "This piece is the foundation. All the pieces rest on this one. When a person is integral, every piece fits together to make a whole. Without integrity the person gathers up role models and tries to copy them. He changes his plans and identity often."

We go on to talk about personality and brokenness. "Each piece is valuable to the function of the cup. During my time with you it will be important to find all the pieces that make up your personality. There are parts of you that you don't know. There are some that do not belong to you at all. Other parts are hidden, and you hope no one finds them. There are presentable parts that anyone can observe. Even the little pieces are important." I then pick up a very small piece. "Without the other broken pieces, there is no way to know what this is. Do you know that many people feel like this little piece? They think they are of no value and belong in the trash." I then throw the piece into my waste-paper basket. (This illustration makes most people very uncomfortable.) Many try to rescue the piece in the garbage. Others just stare at me, as if to say, *"How could you do that?"*

I then drive the point home. "God values you. Tenderly He puts the pieces together. Scars and tell-tale signs of wear and tear are evident. You are not displayed on a shelf to be admired. You, the cup, are designed to hold God's Life. He dwells in vessels set apart for His purposes. From you, His vessel, He pours His Life out to others. God has no dwelling place on earth, no receptacle for His Life except people. You are alive, not an inanimate object, and therefore, restoration continues throughout life as you become more and more the expression of God's Love."

* * *

To Be As A Little Child

We, the followers of the Lord, are to love as He did: to love God, to love ourselves, to love others. The question is — how? The surprising answer — become as a little child.

> Assuredly, I say to you unless you are converted and become as little children, you will by no means enter the Kingdom of Heaven. (Mt.18:3)

Obviously, we are no longer children. How can I become as a little child again? God does the impossible. He helps us leave behind childishness (self-centeredness and defensiveness) and to be childlike.

The beginning point for a Life-giver is *to be,* not to perform, not to be perfect, not to be god-like. We are to be childlike, like we were when we were young. Children are curious, observant, responsive, loving, playful and spontaneous. During our church service I held little ten month old Steven. He was very quiet as he gazed into my face. He watched me and then touched my eyebrows, nose, and mouth. He smiled, and clapped, giggled and laughed as I sang. Finally he nestled into my lap and fell asleep. He was childlike - curious, observant, responsive, loving, playful, and spontaneous. A child simply is. We are *to be.*

The restoration of our childlikeness is part of transformation. Wisdom and knowledge follow. In this way we are conformed to the image of Christ. Jesus started as a baby, a child. He was always secure because of the Father's love. Therefore He was able to be open and vulnerable to others. He had no overlay, no defensiveness, no self-centeredness and no fear. He was fully alive to the Father and to others. Yes, He did suffer, for this is an inevitable part of life as a Life-giver.

How many of us are childlike? Openness and vulnerability are anathema to survival in our society. Yes, if childlike, we may be wounded as Jesus was. We will also be loved as Jesus was loved. In this day and age where many people are too hurried and driven to be open and friendly, vulnerable and caring, it is difficult to find anyone who is childlike. Whoever is willing to pay this price gives Life to others and is like the great Life-giver.

What were you like as a child? See if you can remember a time before you were six, before you became cluttered and complicated. Usually, it is possible to recall a 'thumb nail' sketch of childlikeness. Many have shared their memories with me which reveal the essence of the person.

Friendly and warm in personality one women shared: "It was summer. My brothers and sisters and I jumped from the cab of an old truck into a mattress placed on the ground. I loved the feeling of falling. It was more exciting for me because I was the youngest and smallest in our family. What fun we had!"

Another friend told me: "Very early on a warm summer day, I would go out and pick wild blackberries. I was bare-footed and wore only shorts. I would climb into the black- berry patch on a treasure hunt to find the biggest berries hidden within the vines. I brought the berries to Mom who turned them into pie or cobbler, or berries on ice cream. I loved the quiet gentleness of the morning. It was as if I were returning to the garden of Eden."

Another young man began to laugh as he recalled: "I loved to be alone high up in a tree on a windy day. I escaped chores and mother."

This is one of my memories: "I loved to skate. I jumped off curbs, coasted down hills, yelled and squealed with delight. I was on a wild race to be the fastest skater on earth." Am I like that today? Ask my friends!

Another man told me: "We lived in North Dakota. I loved the storms that blew in from the north. I would get all dressed up in layers of clothes until I could hardly walk. I took my toy gun, went out and played war in the blizzard."

These stories are about 'being' instead of performing. They speak of freedom and joy, vitality and enthusiasm, and quiet solitude. We are robbed of enjoyment and celebration of Life when childlikeness is lost. This is not as it should be. Transformation restores adventure, awareness of others, imagination. Is it possible to be an adult and be childlike? Oh, I hope so!

* * *

Jesus Christ Our Example

> Let this mind be in you which was also in Christ
> Jesus......and coming in the likeness of men. (Phil. 2:7-8)

Jesus' humanity was a cross He had to bear. He was limited by a human body, a human mind, a human personality. Eventually, His human life, a cross, led to the Cross and His death.

Jesus left the heavenly realm of glory, dominion, reputation. He came to us as a bondslave. He left the other place and became man, not a mature man, but a baby...
naked and covered with Mary's blood.

> He had only three things...
> the Father's image deep within.
> a longing, a desire to be with the Father.
> his own uniqueness and destiny.

Jesus was like any other baby: dependent, needy, and unique. This was the cross He carried during his earthly life.

"I will praise you for I am fearfully and wonderfully made. Marvelous are your works..." (Ps.139:14)

HIDDEN
PREPARATION

"And the Child grew and became strong in spirit, filled with wisdom and the grace of God was upon Him." (Lk.2:40)

Children have an incredible ability to learn. Their capacity to hear and duplicate language surpasses ours. A child picks up information from everywhere. We watch in amazement as our baby grows into a child, then a young adult. Skills are learned at phenomenal rates and yet, without wisdom, the child remains emotionally and spiritually immature.

A believer remains a baby, retarded, unable to function when there is no spiritual foundation. There are no short cuts to maturity. The depth of spiritual understanding is directly proportionate to the investment one makes.

Spiritual growth, unlike physical growth, continues throughout a lifetime. We become more like the Lord the longer we know Him. There is an adage that states, "We become what we worship." We take on the Lord's wisdom and character, and yet, do not lose our own personality. In fact, when spiritually mature, we are more at ease, natural and unpretentious.

* * *

Jesus Prepares

The scriptures contain very little about Jesus as a child. We do know He grew in wisdom and stature and in favor with God and man. Jesus learned the lessons of home   as He worked with Joseph, his father. As a carpenter he made common things — tables and chairs, yoke for oxen, tools. The God of Glory lived the ordinary life of a youth.

The love of God and love of others was central to the Hebrews. Life centered around the ancient and scriptural rhythms of daily prayer, weekly Sabbath, and annual celebrations.   Jesus was part of a people with a unique calling and purpose. The Hebrew boys attended Yeshiva to study the writings of Moses and the history of these special people: the chronicles of the Judges and Kings, and the Prophets and the Wisdom literature. They learned of a promised Messiah who would save His people. The written word, basic law, and cultural celebrations and traditions, formed a body of knowledge that built a spiritual foundation.

In the gospel of Luke, chapter two, it is said of Him,

> At the age of twelve Jesus was about His Father's business. He was found sitting in the midst of the teachers, both listening to them and asking them questions. And all who heard Him were astonished at His understanding and answers. (Lk.2:46-47)

God's grace was with Jesus as He grew into manhood. He worshipped, studied, and worked. *He waited*. He suffered all the indignities of being human. He made choice after choice to listen to Father God and do His bidding. Jesus' preparation for His special destiny took thirty years. Thirty years! There were no short cuts. At the end of this time God the Father blessed Him: "This is my Beloved Son in whom I am well pleased!" (Lk.3:22)

* * *

Spiritual Foundation

Thirty years is a long time to prepare for anything. Yet, we are called to prepare for our destiny over a lifetime. All the knowledge of the Word, the rhythms of scripture, and the ordinary lessons of home, are to bring us to know God, who is our destiny.

The fear of the Lord is the beginning of wisdom, and the knowledge of the Holy One is understanding. (Pr.9:10)

The Word Of God As Spiritual Foundation
It is necessary to mark, study, learn, and inwardly digest the Word of God in order to establish a spiritual foundation. There is no other way.

> All Scripture is given by inspiration of God, and is profitable for doctrine, for reproof, for correction, for instruction in righteousness, that the man of God may be complete, thoroughly equipped for every good work. (2Tim.16-17)

Helpful Ways To Hear God Speak As The Bible Is Read
We usually read a book from start to finish to see the plot; enjoy the story; glean information. The Bible contains story, plot, and information, however more importantly, *the Bible is God speaking to you and me.* I have read it for over thirty years and still there is more to understand and learn. One of the most wonderful rich experiences of Life is to have the reading of words become the hearing of His Voice.

When you first start to read the Bible do not get hung up on details. Read a good modern paraphrase for an overview. Then go on to use a good accurate translation of the Bible for more detailed study. Use a study Bible: read introductions to the different books, background information, and word definitions.

Notice God's different attributes. For instance, realize how patient He had been before He brought judgment upon His people. Note His many characteristics all held in tension: His righteousness as well as His mercy; His anger and fury; His tender-hearted love; His sorrow and His joy. Your picture of God may be incomplete if you read only one portion of the Word.

The Bible should be read with questions in mind. A child asks "why" thousands of times. "Why is the sky blue?" "Why do you have bumps (wrinkles) on your face?" "Why does it rain?" "Why, Why, Why?" Anyone who has raised a child laughs and cries at the same time just trying to answer the questions. Curiosity leads to learning and discovery. Our natural inquisitiveness and the desire to know God should motivate us to learn God's word. It is not merely a task to do or a duty to perform. It is a great adventure. It is the only way to know truth, to become wise, to understand spiritual things, and to lay a foundation.

Isolate a theme such as hope, and trace it through all the scripture. Note the prayers. Read and enjoy the stories. Study God's specific commands. Find out why God demands what He does.

When I find it difficult to understand a passage in scripture I go on what I call a treasure hunt. "What does this word mean?" "What is He saying and why?" "How does this apply to what just occurred?" The meaning can be ferreted out by the use of study tools: cross referencing, different translations and paraphrases, dictionary and concordance, a study Bible, and Hebrew and Greek translations. Once I think I understand, I ask God to apply it to my life. Over a period of time, He does. The application leads to more questions and answers and more understanding of scripture.

Become part of the story or scene as you read. Ask questions. "Why did you heal that women and not these?" "What does "poor in spirit" mean? Show me an application." "I don't understand this story; it doesn't seem to fit the circumstance." Again go on a search for Truth. He will meet you and enjoy your company. As you read the epistles apply the truth to your life, church life, or the situation at work. Try it on for size. If it doesn't work, ask why? As you read — Stop! Slow down and think about what you have read. Stop! Pray for understanding. Stop! Experience what you read. Stop! Watch the Lord apply His wisdom to your life. Stop! See your attitude or perception change. The Bible is God speaking to you. Pay attention! Listen! Observe! Pray!

All of the common, general will of God is contained in the scriptures. Directions for everyday life can be found there. I have heard, *"If I just knew what God wanted, I would do it!"* Most of the time the answer is in the Word of God. Your faith will remain superficial if there is no in-depth experiential understanding of scripture. If scripture is read in a hurry to get through it, to finish the book, to find quick and easy direction for the immediate guidance needs, it will not give up its treasure. The treasure of the word is a knowing of the Lord in which we come to have an intimate relationship with him.

I have been deeply grieved when some approach the scriptures casually. They pick and choose what they think is good as if reading a menu. Some are quick to say, "That part of scripture is primitive culture, we are beyond that now." "There must be some mistake, a living God would never slaughter anyone." "The creation story — everyone knows it is just an ancient tale."

The word of God cannot be understood with an attitude of unbelief. It is necessary "to believe that He is, and He is the rewarder of those who diligently seek Him." (Heb.11:6)

The Law as Spiritual Foundation
The ten commandments are the foundation of law and social order. The first section states, "I am the Lord, your God. You shall have no other gods before me." (Ex.20:2-3) Is God the only god in your heart? Examine your priorities. You may be surprised how much worth (worship) is given to other things? How often is His name casually used or used in a curse? Is there a day set aside for the worship of the Lord? What are Sundays like at your house? In what do you trust? Is the great commandment established in your heart? (Ex.20:2-11)

The second section of the law applies to social order. Without God's Law, it is easy to adapt to the ever changing standard of our culture. God's law never changes. It is the standard. The law of God states: honor your father and mother, do not murder, commit adultery, steal, bear false witness, or covet. (Ex.20:12-17)
Jesus summarized the law —

> You shall love the Lord with all your heart, with all your soul, and with all your mind. This is the first and great commandment. And the second is like it: You shall love your neighbor as yourself. (Mt.22:37-39)

Do you want to follow Jesus? Hide the Word in your heart; Obey simple law.

Religious Celebrations and Traditions as Spiritual Foundation
The Hebrews told and retold the story of God's extraordinary intervention in their lives.

"We are the sons of Abraham, Isaac, Jacob. God brought us out of Egypt; gave us a land; sent water out of a rock; fought battles for us; directed us with a pillar of fire and a cloud." (Author's paraphrase)

Three thousand years of history was rehearsed. Why did they do this? It is my opinion that God wanted them to remember the unfolding story of His love. He knew they would forget without this repetition.

God required the Jews to celebrate three main holidays. Their deliverance from Egypt is remembered with the celebration of Passover and the week of Unleavened Bread. The first fruits of the harvest is celebrated fifty days after the barley harvest and is called Pentecost. The end of harvest is celebrated with Trumpets (Rosh Hashanah), Day of Atonement (Yom Kipper), and Taberna- cles (Booths). * Each of these celebrations was to remind the Hebrews of their God who brought them into a land of their own, made them a people called by His name, and blessed them abundantly. They were continually to remember the covenant God had made with them. He was their God; they were His People. Out of this agreement God blessed them for faithfulness, and they reaped death if they were unfaithful and served other gods. The celebrations were entwined inexorably in the rhythm of their lives to reenact God's intervening actions.

If this be true for the Jews, it is also true for believers. Our days of remembrance are Christmas, Easter, and Pentecost. Churches cele- brate these events annually. Why celebrate traditional holidays (Holy days)? Simply because they are holy days; days to remember God's graciousness. Christ's birth, Christmas (Christ Mass), marks the miraculous event when God the Father, gave the World Jesus as a newborn baby. The telling and retelling of this story is to remind us of a God who gives. (I wonder how Santa got the prime-time?)

Easter is a celebration of the great Passover, the slaying of the Lamb of God. Do we prepare with prayer and fasting? Do we stop all our busyness and remember, contemplate, rejoice because Jesus died as the Lamb of God? Do we marvel at the resurrection? Do we embrace the reality of forgiveness and the complete atone- ment for our sin? The celebration of Easter is to tell and retell of

Jesus' death and resurrection, so that no one can ever forget what God has done. However, many find it is easier to believe the folktale of a Easter bunny who lays eggs. (Maybe I have it wrong; I think the bunny brings eggs?)

Pentecost is the celebration of the giving of the Holy Spirit to the church. Without this event, we would not even care about spiritual things. He, the Holy Spirit, is the one who teaches all things, comforts, convicts of sin, empowers, brings fruitfulness, reveals truth in the scriptures, and guides. This is the forgotten story in Acts chapter two.

Jesus also commands us to remember the New Covenant with the breaking of bread and the drinking of the wine. We are to remember the broken Body and Blood of Christ as often as we eat bread and drink the fruit of the vine. Each day, every day, we are to remember, and be thankful for God's great gift of the Son. Holy Communion is a reenactment of God's sacrifice, covenant, fellowship, and brokenness.

Jesus celebrated with the Jews great holidays; we celebrate the holy days of remembrance in order to give Him praise, thanksgiving, repentance, offerings and ourselves. In return, we receive His Life. Times of celebration and remembrance are of great importance and are part of a solid foundation of spiritual life. Oh church, do not forget God's Gift. Do not forget the God of our Fathers, the God who gives Life. Make the Holy Days, Holy Days of remembrance. Remember and celebrate.

Scriptural Rhythms As Spiritual Foundation
Have you ever experienced a daily rhythm of prayer? The monastic orders were governed by a daily prayer discipline. This seems a bit routine and structured, but it is scriptural. Our Christian tradition includes morning and evening prayer, the reading of the scripture, the singing of songs. God instructs us to ask Him to give wisdom to rulers, to heal the sick, to comfort the brokenhearted.

The rhythm of Sabbath, six days of work, the seventh for rest is ancient tradition. The celebration with other believers of God's great Gift of His Son is for our good, for our instruction, for our discipline, and for our spiritual encouragement. Do not forgot the Sabbath, the Lord's Day. It is not your day to spend as you like; it is the Lord's day.

Foundation is set by these rhythms. They are used as vehicles of grace whereby we come to an ever increasing knowledge of God.

Lessons of Home As Spiritual Foundation
What are the lessons we learn at home? You might say we learn everything from home. We learn all habits, attitudes, and philosophy of life. We learn obedience as we listen to instruction from our parents. We learn trust and security, or mistrust and insecurity. Our attitudes about work, diligence, skill, and thoroughness are established at home. Enjoyment of life and ways to play begin here. Good eating habits and patterns of rest are set in place. Celebration of important events such as birthdays, and national and religious holidays create traditions for noting special events. When God is introduced to children at a young age faith in God, prayer, worship, testimony, rejoicing with song are a normal part of growing up. The family is a community who welcomes friends and strangers into the safety of home. It is here the child learns to help the sick, comfort the grieving, and enjoy friends and family.

Many have no healthy home experience. Their natural life cycles have never been established. As a result they don't eat right or get enough rest. They do not work hard and then play or enjoy people and then quiet down in solitude. Everything seems a crisis. They are tossed to and fro without discipline, order, or skill. They then wonder why it is so difficult to grow spiritually.

One summer we cared for several children who needed a home. They had lived on peanut butter sandwiches and an intellectual diet of television. The children were left alone much of the time and had done whatever they pleased. They lived in filth. When they first came to stay with us, they did not want to eat regular food. After a couple of days of no peanut butter, they were glad to eat fresh blueberries, strawberries, carrots, cucumbers, corn, and green beans. They saw the stars at night. They tumbled into bed at nine o'clock tired from a day of work and play. They learned that kids help with the fire wood, wash dishes, pick beans, assist with supper, make beds, and pick up clothes. They swam in the cold creek; it was fun. They learned that frogs croak; dogs are friendly; parents mean what they say; reading is pleasure; music and art are part of life. They laughed and giggled at funny stories told at the dinner table. They built forts on the hill, a dam in the creek, and caught crawdads. They experienced "home."

If you, as with many others, are missing this vital link of "home" as spiritual foundation, it is not too late. Start by simply eating three meals a day of good food. Go to bed and get enough sleep. Find a way to exercise. Get outside and walk in the rain, listen to the sounds, smell the odors, look at the stars. Work when you are at work; do a good job. Read instead of watching television. Listen to good music. Create something: build, draw, sew, plant, or cook. Most of all, *Stop* (quit) running around; plan your week with work and play; rest and celebration; social activity and solitude. These simple disciplines set a tone for life. Without adequate rest, etc. it is impossible to concentrate, much less read the Bible. Without quiet it is impossible to hear the gentle quiet voice of God. He won't compete with the television, VCR's, boom boxes, computer games, or even crunchy potato chips.

"Home" is where we learn all habits, disciplines, skills, and spiritual life.

Personal Life As Spiritual Foundation
The voice of the Holy Spirit invades all of life. He does speak. Is He heard? He sounds very quiet, gentle, confrontive, and truthful. We might hear His quiet voice within, *"Did you pick up your clothes this morning?"* (Sometimes He sounds like mother.) God does train his children to be responsible. Or we may hear, *"That wasn't exactly telling the truth. Why not correct what you just said."* Or He might say, *"You promised to spend time with the kids, why are you watching television?"* Our response is often, *"I'll do it later."* The Holy Spirit has us in school. Do we respond as badly now as when we were kids? All of our excuses must come to an end. He trains us to willingly obey without hesitation. To hear His Voice and obey is foundational.

Unless the Lord is heard when He speaks, He cannot be obeyed. He lives within the Christian. Have you ever experienced the indwelling Christ? Sensing His presence starts with prayer. Prayer is simply an interaction between people and God. To study about prayer misses the point. It should be the natural outflow of an awareness of His Presence. If prayer is a duty, then your relationship with God is a duty, not a loving outflow of communion with Him. Start to practice prayer by offering thanks to God. A child prays very specifically. "Thanks for the spoons, potato, milk, my sister, the sky, my dog, etc." It can go on and on. Try thanking God for five minutes. At first, it will seem a long time. Establish a habit of thanksgiving. "Thanks, Lord for the morning, the sun, warm water, my wife, the kids, the car, etc. Thanks for your love, care, steadfastness, and tender-mercy." All day long thanksgiving should rise to God.

The next step is to ask Him a question. What do you want to know? Be specific. Watch for the answer. It may take time; a week, a month, a year is not too long. Note the answer; write it down. Ask for little things; notice when the answers come. Write them down. It is absolutely necessary to note the answers to prayer. Sometimes life takes a turn for the worse; it is then that rehearsing God's goodness and faithfulness brings hope and encouragement.

Several years ago, I asked the Lord to change my poor communication with my children. Over a period of time He taught me the reasons for my behavior. I learned about my anger and fear, selfishness and laziness, rebellion and discipline. I learned to follow through when I gave an order. The Lord was very thorough. Several years later I realized He had answered my prayer. I no longer yelled at the children to get them to obey.

The establishment of spiritual foundation brings great gain. We do not need to qualify for "ministry" with unusual feats of proficiency in spiritual matters. We must first do simple things while the Father speaks to us. As we are faithful in ordinary life, God gradually removes pretense, selfish ambition and the need for approval. Self confidence is gained as we do the tasks at hand. The fear of failure diminishes as trust in God increases. Jesus prepared for three years of public ministry. Will we follow?

> "...till we all come to the unity of the faith and of the knowledge of the Son of God, to a perfect man, to the measure of the stature of the fullness of Christ; that we should no longer be children, tossed to and fro and carried about with every wind of doctrine — but speaking the truth in love, may grow up in all things into Him who is the head — Christ."(Eph.4:13-14)

Notes:

Section 3
Follow To Establish Foundation

Chapter 6
Image and Desire
The Book of Common Prayer, (New York, New York, The Seabury Press, 1977) p.355

Chapter 7
Deny Yourself
* scepter (Nu.24:17), sword (Ex.21:3) crown (Rev.14:14) robe (Rev.19:13) feet (Gen 3:15)
1 Peterson, *The Message,* p.483
"Where do wars and fights come from among you? Do they not come from your desires for pleasure that war in your members? You lust and do not have. You murder and covet and cannot obtain. You fight and war. Yet you do not have because you do not ask. You ask and do not receive, because you ask amiss, that you may spend it on your pleasures." (Jam.4:1-3 NKJ)

Chapter 8
Your Cross
* Nouwen, Henri J.M., *The Life of the Beloved,* (San Francisco, California, Harper Collins Publ.) This entire book is a wonderful explanation of the Love of God.

Chapter 9
Hidden Preparation
* Passover, Unleavened Bread: Ex.12;1-20, 13: 3-10; Lev.23: 5-8; Nu.9:1-14;28:16-25 Deut.16:1-8
Weeks (Harvest or Pentecost): Ex.23:16;34:22; Lev.23:15-21; Nu.28:26-31; Deut.16:9-12
Trumpets: Lev.23:23-25, Nu.29:1-6
Day of Atonement: Lev.16:23-32 Nu.29:7-11
Tabernacles: Ex.23:16;34:22; Lev.23:33-36,39-43; Num.29:12-38; Deut.16:13-15

FOLLOW HIM
INTO LIFE

"For whoever desires to save his life will lose it,
but whoever loses his life for My sake
and for the gospel's sake will save it.
For what will it profit a man
if he gains the whole world and loses his own soul?
Or, what will a man give in exchange for his soul?
For whoever is ashamed of Me and My words
in this adulterous and sinful generation,
of him the Son of Man also will be ashamed
when He comes in the glory of His Father
with the holy angels."
(Mk.8:35)

WILDERNESS
AND THE TEST

"Then Jesus was led up by the Spirit into the wilderness to be tempted by the devil. And when He had fasted forty days and forty nights, afterward He was hungry. Now when the tempter came to Him, he said, "If You are the Son of God..." (Mt.4:1-3)

The wilderness is the examination room:

> a place of separation
> a place of silence
> a place of solitude
> a place of simplicity
> a place where Satan dwells
> a place where God is silent.

How do you feel when you take a test? Anxious? Afraid? Challenged? Prepared? Be assured, you will be tested as a believer. Why is this necessary? The believer must see how much spiritual foundation is in place. A good test determines authenticity. It shows the student what has become part of his knowledge base, and what has not. The test may be the door to the future, the beginning of 'real life.' A test examines competence. Someone can act like a doctor, yet only a physician who has passed his examinations is licensed to practice. In the same way, a believer may act like a Christian, but after the examination he knows with a certainty who he is and what is true. The believer learns that his faith is authentic. He also knows a great deal more about his hidden motives, addictions, and idols.

We may have a title of honor and authority, but it is our action under testing which establishes authenticity.

* * *

Jesus spent thirty years on earth hidden from public view, and then, in the fullness of time, He was introduced. John the Baptist pointed Him out, "Behold the Lamb of God!" God the Father said, "You are my beloved Son in whom I am well pleased." The Holy Spirit then descended upon Jesus to anoint Him and mark Him as the Son of God. His ministry had begun. The first stopping place was the wilderness where the devil waited.

Jesus had no comfort in this fearsome desert. He was alone, without food or shelter. Silence, solitude, exposure, and hunger set the stage for His time of testing. The devil lived in this place to threaten and harass Jesus. After forty days, the test began:

The examiner, the devil, challenged, "If you are the Son of God?" (Lk.4:1-13)

To even question that Jesus was God's Son was an insult to the Father and the Son. Satan wanted Jesus to rise to the bait. The tempter might have sounded like this: "Make the stones turn into bread. Take care of yourself. Go ahead and end this test and satisfy your flesh. You are hungry. Why suffer when you have the power to fix the situation?"

Jesus, the Beloved Son, remembered the Father's blessing. He remembered all the scriptures that spoke of Him and this time. The Word, The Spirit, and the Father were in agreement. (1Jn.5:7) He was indeed the Messiah. The Father provided everything He needed. Jesus answered, "Man shall not live by bread alone, but by every word of God." (Lk.4:4)

God alone is the source of Life.

The examiner spoke again, "If you want power and glory take it now!" Satan offered the Things of Man. Jesus, the Father's bond-

99

servant, had settled this long ago. All things were left behind in the heavenly realm. Jesus was clothed in humility and meekness, the royal robe of a bondslave. He answered the enemy, "You shall worship the Lord your God, and Him only you shall serve." (Lk.4:8) Worship was the issue.

God alone is worthy of praise.

The examiner, the accuser of the brethren, taunted, "If you are the Son of God...prove it. Go ahead and jump from this high place. How do you know if God meant what He said? Prove it for yourself. Did you really hear the Father call you His Beloved? It is strange that You wander out in the desert." Jesus answered, "You shall not tempt the Lord your God." (Lk.4:12)

God alone is sovereign.

Satan departed. The examination was finished. Jesus had no doubt that He was the beloved Son of the Father. The Father knew ahead of time the Son would not fail the test. This test under the extreme conditions in the wilderness, prepared Jesus for another time to come when He would hang on a Roman cross.

* * *

The Wilderness and the Test
During a lifetime everyone is tempted. The believer must choose between the Things of Man and the Things of God. He must decide the right thing to do. He must continue to be truthful. He knows that those choices lead to Life instead of death. His choices must be based on the standard, the Word of God.

This test in the wilderness is different. The wilderness is not a physical place; it is a desert of the soul. This wilderness (the examination room) is not entered unless it is ordered by the Lord. Here God uses separation, silence, solitude, and simple routine to uncover hidden motives, addictions, and idols. The inner voices of our own flesh and that of the tempter become evident. Within this experience there is a relinquishment of the Things of Man, great grief and struggle, and finally there is rest. God seems to withdraw.

The enemy challenges, "If you are a child of God..." How we respond to this insulting threat determines whether we stand in faith or collapse in faithlessness. In either case the test is not the end. The test reveals our spiritual foundation. God never abandons us; He is not disappointed. He knows ahead of time what needs to change. After the test, we also know. The stress resulting from the wilderness experience causes weakness and fatigue, pain, loneliness, and sorrow.

This experience is difficult to share. If you have been there, you remember vividly the despair. As fearful as this experience is, it is absolutely essential for spiritual growth.

The Wilderness — Separation
The wilderness is marked by sudden, permanent, and disastrous change that separates the believer from ordinary life: a job or location change, physical or emotional break down, death or illness of a family member. This has occurred several times during my adult life. Each time the turn of events was not anticipated and was very stressful. The wilderness is entered alone, separated from anyone or anything.

I recently experienced such an abrupt and painful transition. The situation in the church changed and as a consequence I found myself no longer in public ministry. My plans and focus changed suddenly. I experienced immediate intense loneliness and disorientation. I wrote of this experience of separation in my journal:

This week has been intensely sad and quiet...
> the widow is now separated into another life.
> the prophet rests in the quiet of the desert.
> the teacher remembers the classroom and delights in those
>> who learned — misses the bright conversations, the questions, the sharing, the miracle of insight and growth.
> the lover has no one to treasure and delight in — no one to
>> find — no one to embrace.
> the lamb is caught on a high ledge — the wind, the only noise
>> — the darkness comes quickly. There is no shepherd —
>> there are no sheep.
> the exile belongs nowhere — has no hope of return. Others
>> cry with him; they too are the "rebels," "the enemy."

I feel like a person who is waiting in a train depot. I should know what I am waiting for or whom I am to meet, yet I cannot remember. I seem to have forgotten time and season, purpose and goals. I am just waiting. I feel overwhelmed when someone comes to comfort, bring warmth, food, a touch of love. I am so thankful and appreciate everything so much. The tears come easily when others are thoughtful and kind to me.

I was in shock. All I could do was sit and wonder. I thought about all that had been part of my life. It was a distant memory. God seemed far away. My inner confusion rose to the surface. I wondered, "What is happening to me?"

Separation whether it be from a spouse, a church, a job, a school, a friend, or a community is the entrance price into the wilderness.

The Wilderness — Silence *
A peculiar kind of silence occurs after separation. This silence is a powerful tool used by the Spirit. The separation itself causes deafness. People speak, but all of their kindly advice falls on deaf ears. In the silence the inner cacophony rises: *If only...I should know better...I want...I don't care if it is right...O it would be so good if I could have...I should have tried harder...why is this happening to me?* The loudness of the inner *'I this and I that'* is deafening. The inner conversation is awful.

Hidden in the midst of the inner noise is another message. It is from the enemy. *"No one cares. It makes little difference what you do."*

God is silent.

The Wilderness — No Comfort
The wilderness seems to have nothing in it. The flesh, the outer man, badgers and complains, screams and desires. It wants and needs many things. Addictions are apparent. The desire to run, escape, abandon all, becomes foremost; however there is no place to go.

It is here that you and I learn how important ordinary things have become: food, work, money, a soft bed, hot shower, and clean clothes. How important is entertainment: reading material, television, Monday night football, and the computer? This place "without" uncovers dependency upon things and people.

Idolatry becomes very clear. God is important, but so are things. God alone is not enough. The idols are evident. An idol is anything that competes with God for undivided affection: a friend, spouse, job, project, or a child. These loves must be relinquished. This is not easy. Maybe your experience is not like mine, but I do not want to let go for I just might have to do without them. I hate this place. God is uncompromising. You and I must worship only God. A jealous God commands,

> I am the Lord your God...You shall have no other gods before Me. (Ex.20:2-3)

Relinquishment of all, causes deep agonizing grief. The job, the position, the challenges, the money, the busyness, the hope and dreams invested in life, are gone. These loves must belong to the Lord. You wonder and ask, "Will they be returned?" I'm not sure. Tears, anger, depression, fatigue, sickness, despair are the daily portion. The silent scream, "Why?!" goes unanswered. Prayer is pain-filled. It now expresses the groans of the broken-hearted.

The Father knows the pain. He watches the struggle to place Him first. At last the battle is over. He then hears the tearful confession. He comforts and heals. He forgives. He instructs. He takes the clutter and accumulated unrighteousness from the inner core. He speaks gently, quietly, *"Be still...and know...that I am God."* (Ps.46:10) Separation, silence, and discomfort are powerful tools.

The Wilderness — Solitude *
The wilderness is a place of solitude. Here there are no others. The test is for you, alone. No one will come here with you. The battle is yours; the victory will be yours. We usually fear solitude because it opens the inner chaos.

Thoughts center on what others think when approval from people is extremely important. *"I wonder if he...I sure hope they think...I don't want to disappoint them...They won't like me if I say the wrong thing...If I act interested they will...She seems to like me...They never told me anything positive, that is why I'm critical and negative...If I don't say anything, then they won't..."*

When people are no longer present, there is no one to tell me who I am, and how I am doing, no one to copy or react against. Here I must go without admiration and praise. In solitude you and I must face our inner emptiness. *"Is anyone home inside?"*

Solitude assists me to hear God. He can affirm the real person. He alone knows my inner thoughts and desires. He loves the simple person; the one who is childlike. He is not interested in my superficial facade. It is essential that I put an end to all the complicated systems I have invented to feel good about myself. The Father delights in me, yet the question remains, do I agree with Him?

The Wilderness — Simplicity *
Now imagine yourself in a desert wilderness. This trip will give you a mind picture of life in an environment where everything is different and simplified. The night is dark and cold. Daylight comes early. It is so quiet; there is no sound at all except the inner "static on the line."(inner conversations about everything essential and non-essential) Life narrows into a simple routine. Since there is no food to eat, breakfast is finished before it starts. Minutia drifts into the mind. The word, learned in another time and season, may be remembered.   There is no energy to do anything. We might play "throw the rocks" for awhile or sing a song or two. Would you like that? All right, let's take a walk, but where is there to go? We nap in the shade of a rock.(there are no trees) We think some more. We pray for everyone that comes to mind. We wander.

We begin to *see* the desert: the shape of the rocks, the deep shades of color, the sun, the illusions of water, the unending expanse of sky. Then the darkness, sudden and dense, closes out even our surroundings. The closeness of the black velvet of sky, the millions of stars tells us about infinite things we cannot even begin to understand. We question, meditate and wonder about life, death, creation, the universe, the beauty of the earth and all the glorious life upon it. And then...thoughts of His Majesty. He is present in this lonely quiet place — without.

Separation, silence, solitude, and simple routine are the Lord's tools to get our attention. The Lord waits until we are ready for the test. When boredom, fatigue, hunger, loneliness, and confusion threaten to overwhelm what is left of our faith, the test comes.

The Wilderness — The Test

The examiner, the devil, pronounces the challenge, "If you are a child of God..."This challenge is an insult. The examiner might sound like this, "Why not just quit? Belief has brought you only grief. Come, walk away. No one would notice or care."

What is your answer?
It is time to remember the God of the scriptures.

> Remember — the historical record, his great acts
> and covenants.
> Remember — the Lord is good.
> Remember — His mercy, His steadfastness.
> Remember — He hides you in the cleft of the Rock.
> Remember — He is a high tower, a fortress in time
> of trouble.
> Remember — what He has done.
> Remember — when you were newborn, forgiven, filled
> with the Spirit, healed.
> Remember — where you have come from.
> Remember — how far you have come.

The answer? "Man shall not live by bread alone, but by every word of God." (Lk.4:4)

God alone is the source of Life.

The examiner, the tempter, asks, "Do you want to be important, to make a difference?"

What is your answer? "Oh, that has been settled already. I am a bondslave of the Father. What I want to be or not to be does not matter. I am at His disposal."

God alone is worthy of praise.

The examiner, the accuser of the brethren, demands, "If you really are a child of God why does God neglect you? You must have done something wrong. If you were loved you would be "blessed." Your faith has failed to bring results."

What is your answer? "I am not afraid. He has redeemed me. He has called me by name. I belong to Him. When I pass through the water, He is with me. And through the rivers, they shall not over-flow me. When I walk through the fire, I shall not be burned, nor shall the flame scorch me. For He, the Lord my God the Holy One of Israel, is my Savior." (Is.43:1-3)

God alone is sovereign. He is the I AM.

The examination is finished. God gently restores ordinary life, yet life is never the same. Tested under extreme conditions, you and I now know that we *know* the Lord.
> God alone is the source of Life.
> God alone is worthy to be praised.
> God alone is sovereign. He is the I AM.

> We also know that "neither death nor life, nor angels nor principalities nor powers, nor things present nor things to come, nor height nor depth, nor any other created thing, shall be able to separate us from the love of God which is in Christ Jesus our Lord." (Rom.8:38-39)

It is God who put you in the wilderness. This experience is usual-ly not a one time test. It can occur daily, or once in a while. The process is the same. The requirement of relinquishment is always present. Idols become evident. The challenge from the enemy is an insult, "If you are a child of God..." I hope you will remember the "Wilderness and the Test" for at least you will recognize the ter-rain.

* * *

> Several years ago I was happily raising a family, in min-istry, enjoying life, when quite suddenly things changed. After a routine physical exam, I faced a diagnosis of sus-pected cancer and surgery. Within a week our family dealt with my possible death, the likelihood of long term illness, and loss of income. Grief permeated our home. Fear dominated my thoughts. We sorted out priorities.

> Major surgery and a long recovery period placed me in the wilderness. I could not read, concentrate, exercise, socially interact, or work. Unable even to pray, others car-ried the burden for my recovery.   I hated this experi-ence. However, God had a reason for all of it.
> He taught me to rest. It was time for our family to learn

once again the temporary and fragile nature of life. We experienced God's love. With my public ministry gone, my health gone, my ability to learn gone, my social contacts gone, what remained? For a while, the place seemed to be empty, but gradually I came to accept that place of nothingness. God had not left me. He was quietly present, not speaking, not instructing, not correcting. Idleness was tremendously painful. Finally, life settled into simple routine. My life was secure with Him. I had to release all other matters. In the process I left behind the idols of work, ministry, people, and the ability to learn. Because of this time in my life, I learned that God is always present.

* * *

Do we become shriveled and barren under testing? If so, the story does not end with failure. The Spirit puts us back in school to learn the basics. If however, our roots have grown deep into God, reflecting none of the barrenness of our circumstances, we are ready to continue to know more of His Majesty.

In the wilderness we come to recognize our hidden attitudes and motives. Our idolatry is evident. Priorities are sorted out. Value is placed upon eternal things. We learn about the love of a Father who releases His children to be tested. In this place of separation, we grow in our 'knowing' of the Lord. As we know Him, we worship Him. A miracle then occurs — We become like the One we worship.

> Cursed is the man who trusts in man and makes flesh his strength, whose heart departs from the Lord. For he shall be like a shrub in the desert, and shall not see when good comes, but shall inhabit the parched places in the wilderness, in a salt land which is not inhabited.

> Blessed is the man who trusts in the Lord, and whose hope is the Lord. For he shall be like a tree planted by the waters, which spreads out its roots by the river, and will not fear when heat comes; but its leaf will be green, and will not be anxious in the year of drought, nor will cease from yielding fruit.
> (Jer. 17:5-8)

ARENA OF
CONFLICT

"The time is fulfilled and the kingdom of God is at hand. Repent, and believe in the gospel." (Mk. 1:15)

It is exciting when special friends come to visit. The house is cleaned from top to bottom. The silver and good dishes are set out for the special meals. The guest room is made ready with flowers, the linen changed. I remember as a child waiting anxiously by the window watching the street. When our friends finally arrived I would shout, "Here they are! Oh, they are finally here!" Our guests received hugs and kisses and greetings of "Welcome. It is so good to see you!" Life took on a holiday atmosphere. Work was put aside during this special time with these friends.

* * *

Now if visits of loved ones can stir us to excitement, imagine the excitement when the advanced messenger of the King cried out, "Hear yea! Hear yea! Repent and be baptized for the Kingdom of God is at hand!" They remembered the scripture in Malachi:

> Behold, I send My messenger, and he will prepare the way before Me. And the Lord, whom you seek will suddenly come to His temple, even the Messenger of the covenant, in whom you delight. Behold, He is coming...But who can

endure the day of His coming? And who can stand when He appears? For He is like a refiner's fire and like launderers' soap. (Mal 3:1-2)

John the Baptist urgently warned, "Pay attention. Pay attention. The mighty Messiah is here! This One will baptize you with the Holy Spirit and fire. His winnowing fan is in His hand, and He will thoroughly clean out His threshing floor, and gather His wheat into the barn; but He will burn up the chaff with unquenchable fire." (Lk.3:16-17)

Jesus, the Son of God, was already in the crowd.

John's life itself marked the end of the old covenant; his warning marked the way into the new covenant. The King was present and in control. He demanded allegiance. Everyone needed to change. Seems easy enough. However, change does not come easily. Everywhere people were in an uproar. Some believed; others did not. Jesus challenged, "This is war, and there is no neutral ground. If you're not on my side, you're the enemy; if you're not helping, you're making things worse." 1 (Mt.12:30) Going into the synagogue in Nazareth, his home town, He made this claim:

> The Spirit of the Lord is upon Me, because He has anointed Me to preach the gospel to the poor; he has sent Me to heal the brokenhearted, to proclaim liberty to the captives and recovery of sight to the blind, to set at liberty those who are oppressed; to proclaim the acceptable year of the Lord...Today this scripture is fulfilled in your hearing."(Is.61:1-2, Lk.4:17-19)

They heard His gracious words, but asked, "Isn't this Joseph's son?" They refused to believe. They attempted to murder Him. (Lk.4:21,28-30)

Jesus' claim to be the I AM made His enemies furious. Controversy and conflict, resistance and hostility followed him everywhere. For example:

> A man who had been struck speechless by an evil spirit was brought to Jesus. As soon as Jesus threw the evil tor-

109

menting spirit out, the man talked away just as if he'd been talking all his life. The people were up on their feet applauding; 'There's never been anything like this in Israel!' The Pharisees were left sputtering, 'Hocus pocus. It's nothing but hocus pocus. He's probably made a pact with the Devil.' 2 (Mt.9:33-34)

There was a man there with a crippled hand. They said to Jesus, 'Is it legal to heal on the Sabbath?' They were baiting him. He replied, 'Is there a person here who, finding one of your lambs fallen into a ravine, wouldn't, even though it was a Sabbath, pull it out? Surely kindness to people is as legal as kindness to animals!' Then he said to the man, 'Hold out your hand.' He held it out and it was healed. The Pharisees walked out furious, sputtering about how they were going to ruin Jesus. 3 (Mt.12:9-14)

The simple people believed and became more and more convinced of his greatness and majesty. The good news spread. Jesus claims were true. He was indeed the I AM, the long expected Messiah. Truth personified spoke of the Father, of Himself, of men's hearts, of coming events. Jesus gained the beach-head into the darkened, alienated, hardened, ignorant hearts of men. Truth broke down the lies and deception within man's minds. Jesus challenged them to believe and leave behind the kingdom of man. Truth was at war with deception. Truth was in opposition to man's opinions.

The Arena of Conflict Consists Of —
The Kingdom Of God —Versus —The Kingdom Of Man

Believers became truth-bearers. As the good news of the kingdom spread, His followers, filled with the power of God, experienced the same warfare and hostility. They too were hated and opposed. There was no middle ground. Each disciple tasted the sting of opposition as the Truth was shared. "Hear yea! Hear Yea! The King is Here!"

Stephen, one of the early believers, lost his life in this arena. We tune in to the end of Stephen's one and only sermon:

110

You stiff-necked and uncircumcised in heart and ears!
You always resist the Holy Spirit; as your fathers did, so do
you. Which of the prophets did your fathers not perse-
cute: And they killed those who foretold the coming of
the Just One, of whom you now have become the betray-
ers and murderers, who have received the law by the
direction of angels and have not kept it." When they
heard these things they were cut to the heart, and they
gnashed at him with their teeth. But he, being full of the
Holy Spirit, gazed into heaven and saw the glory of God,
and Jesus standing at the right hand of God, and said,
'Look! I see the heavens opened and the Son of Man
standing at the right hand of God!' Then they cried out
with a loud voice, stopped their ears, and ran at him with
one accord; and they cast him out of the city and stoned
him.(to death) (Ac. 7:51-58)

We Find The Two Elements In The Arena Of Conflict:
  The Truth (the Kingdom of God).
  The Resistance to the Truth (The Kingdom Of Man)

When truth is spoken, resistance follows. This is the Arena of
Conflict.

* * *

The Battle Of The Kingdoms
We do not live in biblical times, yet the Arena of Conflict continues. When God descends into human affairs there is always resistance. Why is this so? It is because man wants control of his kingdom. Even when good things are offered, man holds on to the
familiar rather than receive something else. Today and each day,
the Messenger, the Holy Spirit, goes before King Jesus, "Repent!
Prepare your heart for the King's entrance. The Kingdom of God
is here, right now! Believe the good news!" Although this call is
heard at the time of conversion, it also is the voice of the Spirit
calling to us. Each day, each hour, each minute a battle rages within our hearts. The Kingdom of God is God's way; the kingdom of
man is my way. They are opposed to each other. The Arena of
Conflict within the human heart is where the battle takes place.

Suppose each day is unpleasant and stressful because you cannot get along with a hateful, unkind person. There seems to be no solution. Nothing ever improves. You cannot leave the situation nor can you straighten it out. The Holy Spirit speaks a word to you, *"Love your enemy."* This command is clearly right and true. Because you desire to be obedient to the word, you try to love this unlovable person. Nothing comes of it because conflict resides in you. You really don't want to love the enemy. No one can see or hear the battle, the hidden conflict. You are the arena.

The inner voice might sound like this: *"No one thinks I can do anything right! I'd like them to try to love that jerk. They think I'm not trying, but I am. I just can't keep it together. My temper is always right there. Why try, it won't work anyway. No one understands what I mean. No one will listen. I'm not to blame.. I hate this. I hate people who think they know when they really don't. God, people are so inconsiderate and thoughtless. I'm going to tell him (the enemy) off the next time I see him. It serves him right. Stop! This is getting nowhere. Maybe I'm the problem. I seem to be at odds with everyone. I'm such a coward. No I'm not. I'm the one that is right. He is just plain wrong."*

The gentle word of the Lord comes underneath the clatter, *"I AM present. Stop all of this and listen? Do you believe the good news (the King is here and in control)? Repent, change your mind and believe the good news. Stop arguing. Get out beyond your opinions, your anger. Pay attention, pay attention! Let me have your right to be right. My wisdom is different from yours."*

Is the enemy the one who makes you miserable? Who is the real enemy? The internal conflict continues: *"No one understands. I never get my way. I won't put up with this any longer. How can I just go without? Maybe a drink would help? No...No that's not right."*

The quiet voice speaks again, *"Come, repent."*

"Why should I repent? I haven't been inconsiderate and thoughtless."

"Is all of this coincidence?"

"Go away. I cannot and won't love that jerk!"

God is silent...

"Why should I? Don't even suggest it. I'm not like him. How can you love him? He is worthless."

"Who is the enemy? Am I? Believe that I AM and I reward those who seek me!"

"God, I hate this place. All the confusion and conflict. I thought being a Christian would be full of blessing."

"It is! You are in conflict with my Kingdom. Come learn from me, I AM meek and lowly of heart."

"You can't love him."

"Yes, I do as I also love you. Love him like I love you."

"Why?"

"Because as you love, you will be loved. As you judge, you will be judged. As you forgive, you will be forgiven. As you are merciful, you will receive mercy. As you desire to do what is right, you will become part of the Kingdom of God."

"This is not fair. He is the one who is wrong, and yet, all of this is about me. Why does he make me so angry? All I feel is anger, hatred, impatience, wants and needs, pride. The real enemy must be my demand to be acknowledged. I have a terrible need to be right. I talk about it, threaten with it. Love, I don't even know what it is. I'm a little dictator ruling my tiny kingdom with criticism and hatred. I act like the one I thought to be my enemy."

"My love for you will heal. I want you to know yourself as I do. The good as well as the bad."

"Oh —

Oh — I see!

I must love the enemy because I am the enemy! I am to love as
you love. I don't know how! God — where do I begin?"

The Arena of Conflict —
The Kingdom of God — TheKingdom Of Man In Conflict.

Human nature resists truth. There is a choice each time truth is
spoken. Will I submit to God and learn his way, or will I just go
ahead and forget it? The arena of conflict does bring great insight.
Truth is His way.

As I have written this manuscript, I have experienced this arena. I
have invested much thought, time and energy into this project.
When others criticized my work, even when they were right and I
knew it, everything in me said, *"No I won't change it; it is mine*
and I like it." After the initial resistance to the truth, the wrestling
began. *"Is the criticism true? If it is true, then what am I going*
to do about it? Should I correct it, rewrite the chapter, start over,
or just quit?" If I resist the truth and do nothing, the thing (manuscript) will never satisfy me. I now know it is not finished. This
makes me mad. The truth of the criticism has a life of its own.
Once spoken it is a burr under the saddle. I have to come to
terms with it and commit to change. I know this principle well; it
does not soften the reaction. You just try writing a book. It
revealed much about my resistance to truth. My loving editors
reaped the negative resistance, then watched me struggle to fix
whatever was wrong. Eventually I was thankful for the truth.

The Arena of Conflict is a real experience. Jesus spoke truth, and
as a consequence, man resisted Him. This deeply grieved Him. He
was a man of sorrows and acquainted with grief. He knows that if
you or I reject Him, fail to repent and believe the good news, we
remain unchanged. He offers Life. Do you continue to receive it?

If we love as He did, and if we carry Truth as He did, then we too
will experience resistance. Believers will be in direct conflict
with the kingdom of man. The miraculous power of God comes
with a price. Some believe and change. Some do not and then we
are the enemy. Like Jesus, we feel the sting of rejection. This
comes as a surprise. We think that if we do a good job, speak the

114

truth, and stay obedient to the Lord, all will go well.
This is not the case.

The Arena Of Conflict — Truth And Conflict Go Hand In Hand

It took me several years to realize this. Whenever God did a marvelous work, there was no end of misunderstanding, conflict and persecution. I decided to try to avoid all this turbulence by not saying much, hedging on the truth, withholding what I knew to be true. This brought an immediate rebuke from the Lord, *"You are becoming self-righteous, and if I give you something to do and say, you had better be obedient!"* He knew that there was no way to avoid this kind of conflict and rejection.

Remember that Jesus commanded us to follow Him. He did not say it would be easy, nor did He say it would make us happy. He followed the Father's command in spite of the cost. If we follow in His steps we will see the power of God at war with all who oppose it. We have the most wonderful privilege to participate in God's presence — His mercy — His healing — His hope — His joy — His passion — His power — His anger — His righteousness — and His suffering!

The Arena of Conflict is continuous. If we pay attention to the internal struggle, we will learn to see not only ourselves, but others with His perception and love. We also will grow in our ability to penetrate the darkness of man's deceptions with the truth.

* * *

Let me share my first experience in the arena. My husband and I began to teach the youth in our church. We were in our mid-twenties with three kids of our own. When we began, these normal teens were more interested in drawing pictures, writing notes, and cutting up in confirmation class, than in deep discussions of religious matters. However, God had His own agenda for us all.

The book of Romans was our starting point. We bravely declared that God wanted to do miracles 'just like in the Bible.' Their response was, *"Put up or shut up!"* We were new born and filled with the Spirit, young and untried in the faith. We shared our personal experience. The Spirit of God moved upon these ordinary teens. They prayed. He answered. They responded and were new born and filled with the Spirit. They loved to pray, sing, worship, and study the scriptures. God was real to them. They were changed.

They talked to and brought their friends, their teachers, their parents to the classes and prayer meetings. Almost every kid in the church received the Lord, and most of their friends came to know the Lord also. The high school changed. The families changed. The church changed. We changed. The Lord was present.

However what I have shared with you about the Arena of Conflict is true. As glorious as His presence was, the resistance and opposition to all of this was incredible. The conflict started in my inner thoughts. *"What will the parents think of this? What if this is not right? We didn't intend to stir up trouble!* My need for approval from others, and my fear of rejection, caused me to wrestle within myself. Was I willing to be labeled different, radical, a religious fanatic? Would I pay the price? I now doubt that I had that choice. God was not pleased with my fretting; He would have none of it. He continued to save, empower, call to ministry, and deliver. Worst of all He used me. (It was wonderful, at the same time it was terrifying.)

Not only was the conflict internal to me, those who did not believe this was of God were irate, organized, frustrated, and extremely hostile. Intense confrontational meetings were held. We were told: "This is not how we do it in this church!" "Where are all these kids coming from? They certainly aren't from here!" "Our rummage sale has been here for years; we need the room." "No one is qualified to lay hands on anyone except the priest." "You must be a cult; it is all hysteria; my child won't participate in this foolishness." "Anyone believing ALL the Bible is certainly ignorant!" "Where have you received your seminary training?" "By what authority can you say such narrow and untrue things as 'Jesus is the only way of salvation?' That simply is not true; what about all the nice people?

God wouldn't send them to hell."

The accusations never stopped. In the end we were told that only the 'pastor' was qualified to teach the class. "We could take the kids bowling and things like that. No more prayer meetings, no more private prayer with the kids, no more 'radical' teaching." The kids all left. We cried.

We wanted to leave this church also. God had another idea. He left us in this congregation to pray, to bless the enemy, to become invisible. His intention for us was spiritual maturity. We learned obedience.

* * *

To be used of God is an incredible privilege and responsibility. The blessing is a mixture of joy and sorrow, love and rejection. God is very present to encourage us to continue to be Life-givers. We must listen to the Father for it is His intention and desire to bring the Truth to us, to change us into "the likeness of His Son."

"Come, Follow Me! The cost is great."

Jesus gave His Life..

Will I follow and lay down my life in the Arena of Conflict?

Is it worth it? Oh, Yes!

> "For those who live according to the flesh set their minds on the things of the flesh, but those who live according to the Spirit, the things of the Spirit. For to be carnally minded is death, but to be spiritually minded is life and peace. Because the carnal mind is enmity against God; for it is not subject to the law of God, nor indeed can be. So then, those who are in the flesh cannot please God." (Rom.8:5-8)

T H E
M O D E L

"You call Me Teacher and Lord, and you say well, for so I am. If I then, your Lord and Teacher, have washed your feet, you also ought to wash one another's feet. For I have given you an example, that you should do as I have done to you." (Jn. 13:3-16)

You, my reader might say, "I've heard about God's love all my life and still I have never experienced it. I'm not even sure what it would be like. Yes, I know about His marvelous gift, His death on the cross for me. Even so, disparity exists between what I believe, and what I have experienced. I hate to tell you this, but sometimes I think God is just an idea in my head, like a distant famous relative whom I have never seen nor known. I'm tired of trying to love. At best I can love when I feel good, but forget it when I am tired, grumpy, or stressed."

Would you like to experience His love? Let me try to introduce you to Him and His incredible, extravagant love.

Come to Passover dinner with the King. You are invited; be yourself. (You may be surprised to find the disciples much like yourself.) Participate. Make comments. See if you can see how to love as the King loves.

* * *

The servant King filled with the Father's love, left the crowd behind and had supper with his friends. He knew them well and loved each one. They came to this Passover with many questions and arguments. They bragged and made wild promises. They asked to see the Father and sit at God's right hand. Strangely enough, Jesus enjoyed their company. He exclaimed, "With fervent desire I have desired to eat this Passover with you before I suffer...(Lk.22:15)

The broken unleavened bread, the wine, the bitter herbs, symbolized the story of God's protection and deliverance of His people. During the supper Jesus took the unleavened bread — broke it — and said, "This is My body broken for you..." He took a cup of wine, "This is My blood of the new covenant." The Lamb of God gave them the symbols of His Love, a broken body and blood poured out as a sacrifice. They participated, yet did not understand. He spoke, "A new commandment I give you, that you love one another as I have loved you."(Jn13:34) I AM — showing you the Father's extraordinary love. I AM — that Love. You are to share Love with others.

Enter the upper room, watch and listen as perfect Love is fully given. See the Father's love. Watch Jesus. Oh, please come into this intimate place where the Son is pouring out the Father's love to his little children, his friends. For here we see Love Incarnate.

They were well into dinner when the servant King Jesus knelt before His friends and washed their feet. They had not bothered with this customary ritual because there was no servant present. The disciples never thought to wash the feet of the King. Jesus cast aside His entitled honor, abandoned status, and washed the dirt from their feet. His tender devotion taught them a new way, the way of Love. Would you have thought to wash the feet of the King? All the feet are dirty, whose feet will you wash?

Jesus knelt before each —
"Peter, take off your sandals."

"You're not going to wash my feet, not mine, never! "

"Peter...if I don't wash your feet you will have no part of me."

"In that case, Lord, wash my whole body!"

"No...Peter, you only need the feet washed. Simon Peter, Satan has asked if he may sift you as wheat. But I have prayed for you, that your faith should not fail; and when you have returned to Me, strengthen your brethren." (Jn.13:6-9 author's paraphrase)

"Lord, I am ready to go with You, both to prison and to death!"

"I tell you Peter, the rooster shall not crow this day before you will deny three times that you know Me." (Lk.22:31-32)

Jesus loved pretentious, self assertive Peter.

As you watch, are you thinking? *"How can He love that brash, boisterous braggart?"* Of course we know that He does. His love is different than ours.

The others listened and watched. They thought they were better than Peter. "We will never leave you, no sir. We will follow you at any cost!" (Mt.26:35 author's paraphrase)

Jesus knew better. All of them would abandon Him, yet eventually all His disciples would suffer because of Him. He knows you will suffer too if you love as He does.

He so loved each one even though they would all leave Him.

Continuing, Jesus knelt before Judas Iscariot — "One of you will betray me. It would have been good if that man had never been born."

"Rabbi, is it I?" .

"You have said it."

Jesus took a piece of bread and dipped it and gave it to Judas — Judas ran from Jesus's love. It was night. (Mt. 26:21-25 author's paraphrase)

Jesus was betrayed. Love was left behind. Jesus, sorrowful and grieved, continued to love this one.

120

You might wonder if you too might betray him. I think under the right circumstances we all might. Even though Jesus did everything right, He was betrayed, yet He loved anyway. His way is quite different than ours, isn't it?"

The disciples each asked, "Is it I?" "Is it I?" "How could anyone betray you, Lord? We would never do that!" (Mt.26:22 author's paraphrase) They did not fully realize their own proclivity to betray.

The Lord knew they were going to run for cover, and yet He loved them.

He moved to other disciples. The sandals off, the feet washed —

They asked, "Tell us who will be the greatest in the coming Kingdom?"

"Why do you dispute about who will be the greatest in the coming Kingdom? Understand — this Kingdom is different. He who is greatest among you, let him be as the younger, and he who governs as he who serves. For who is greater, he who sits at the table, or he who serves? Is it not he who sits at the table? Yet I am among you as the One who serves..." (Lk. 22:24-27)

He loved even these who wanted to be the most important...the position seekers.

Jesus washed John's feet. "My beloved John — You have seen, heard, touched, and known my love. Write what you know. Many will believe because of you. Your testimony of Me will transcend time and the earthly realm." (Rev. 1:17-19 author's paraphrase)

He loved this young man.

Jesus knelt again — "Ah, Philip!"

"Show us the Father, and it is sufficient for us,"

"Philip, have I been with you so long, and yet you have not known Me? He who has seen Me has seen the Father..." (Jn. 14:8)

God, Himself knelt right in front of Philip; He washed and dried his feet. Philip was spiritually blind, unable to see the Father.

Jesus loved this disciple who could neither see, hear, nor understand.

"Thomas — Let not your heart be troubled; you believe in God believe also in Me..."

"Lord, it is difficult to believe any of this. I hear the words but they make no sense."

He gave the Father's gentle love to the troubled and the unbelieving making belief possible.

Judas (not Iscariot) was next —

"How can you manifest yourself to us and not to the world?"

"If anyone loves Me, he will keep My word; and My Father will love him, and We will come to him and make Our home in him. The Father will send the Helper, the Holy Spirit. He will teach you all things and bring to your remembrance all things that I said to you. Peace I leave with you, My peace I give to you."(Jn.14:22-27)

Jesus loved this disciple and the others.

Jesus' good-bye gifts were love, joy, peace, and the Holy Spirit.

Unfortunately the disciples were occupied with the things of man: confusion, fear, ambition, pride, self-assertion, betrayal, unbelief, blindness, sorrow, and grief. They tried to understand, but not grasping His Love, they missed His good-bye.

* * *

Now step out of scripture into real life. Jesus loves us just as He did the twelve. My friend, let me share with you about His Love. I so want you to enjoy His Presence. With the help of the Spirit, He will come and pour His extravagant Love into you. You in turn will respond and love as He Loves.

*It is impossible to give His Life to others until we are loved —
loved by Love Himself.*

If we are preoccupied and our hearts are closed, we too will miss
His love. The symptoms of a closed heart are: regret of past mistakes, fear for the future, criticism of others, and accusation of ourselves. God does not inhabit these places. Until we take our eyes
off ourselves, look up, and welcome the servant King, all the
aspects of His love will be beyond our grasp.

He softly knocks. A lukewarm person does not hear Him at all.
He waits for a passionate focused invitation — *"Lord, come in
and show me why I am far from you, why I can't receive your
love?"*

The Father answers — "As many as I love, I rebuke and chasten.
Therefore be zealous and repent. I stand at the door and knock.
If anyone hears My voice and opens the door, I will come in to
him and dine with him, and he with Me." (Rev.3:19-21)

"Oh Lord, please come in!"

He kneels and washes feet. We may be anxious for an easy
answer, sympathy or revenge. He, instead, addresses the root of
the problem, speaking the truth without condemnation. Nothing
can be hidden. He reveals our own unbelief and self-absorption.
Confession is met with mercy and love. His forgiveness brings
release from shame and despair. Love Himself touches the deep
wounded places. *In failure His love becomes real.* He covers us
with His Love.

> I have always been amazed at the freedom that comes from
> His love. I wrote of this in my journal:
> His love, a burning fire, purifies motives and attitudes.
> His love, honest and yet comforting, wounds and heals.
> His love, deep and strong, breaks down walls of fear, embraces
>   the terrified.
> His love penetrates hearts imprisoned by human designs
>   and plans, breaks control and judgment of others.

His love, filled with joy, expands and splashes all with
　　　encouragement and reaches the inner person and
　　　gives it form and language.
His love, rich, lavish and generous, causes deep longing for
　　　fulfillment and wholeness.
His love gives courage to run the wild race to attain the high
　　　call of God.
His love arms us to do battle with the giants of life.
His love, precious beyond words, very personal, intimate, is
　　　a treasure.

It is good, oh so good to be loved. In exchange for fear He gives
His love. In exchange for hatred He gives His love. In exchange
for anger He gives His love. Peace settles into the soul. Joy
springs forth in laughter, dancing and praise. It is good to be loved
by Love Himself.

Then quietly yet firmly He invites us to kneel in front of His
friends (your boss, your children, your wife or husband, your most
despised associate, your friend) and love as He loves. Peter is waiting. Judas the betrayer may still be there. Andrew, James, John the
beloved, Philip, Thomas, Judas and the others are waiting, also.

Some of us would jump up and say, "Sure, where's the water? Anyone can wash feet." Or a few might be shy, "I just can't." Others
express frustration, "Just tell me how...and then I
will do it!"

Jesus commands us to Love one another as He has loved us. It is
impossible for us to love as He loves. However, He provides the
way. God, already in residence within believers, anxiously desires
to remove our blocks to the outflow of His Love. To act loving is
not the same as to be loving. His Love is a natural outflow of His
Life.

The Outflow of His Love — His Life
His Love reflects His Image.
He places a desire deep within to know Him and to love as He
loves. The search for this love leads to the Servant King.

His Love comes to us first. We respond and then
can love with His Love.

Do you know Jesus as the servant King? He touches, listens to questions, washes the dirt from your feet (all the filth picked up from life.) His touch brings Life. It is impossible to just sit there. Worship, praise, thanksgiving pour out as a natural response. He does not expect you to love without first being loved. He will answer your cry, *"Oh God, Oh God, show me your love!"*

Love cannot be learned from a book. The Holy Spirit, the one sent to accompany us, knows how to love. He turns life into a class- room where everyday events reveal the Father's love in action. Just this week I received three unexpected phone calls and two letters, each one bearing the same message. "God told me to encourage you. I am praying for you." I was thus provided with more than enough evidence to be assured that the Lord was send- ing His love to me via His other friends. If we have eyes to see, we will observe and rejoice in the evidence of God's love.

His Love reflects the Father's love.
The Father loves the Son; the Son loves the Father. The Holy Spirit who loves the Father and the Son, is a dynamic Life-giving Spirit. He dwells within the believer. He is Love. Do you know the Spirit who is powerful, intimate, intense, honoring, and Life-giving? Issue the invitation — *"Spirit of God, please come in power and let me experience first hand the intimacy and love of the Godhead."*

His Love flows outward to others.
Jesus did not say, "Now I have washed your feet, it is time to wash mine." Oh no! His love is given with no strings attached. He tries neither to possess nor to control the one loved. In other words, I am free to receive His Love without my ever giving anything in return. He will still love me; that is His nature. His Love flows outward.

I cannot expect a return when I love as He did. An expectancy of return immediately stops the flow of His Love. Those without His Love might say, "Now that I have loved you, you must love me in return." This is not His way. His kind of love does not keep a tally. It is only as we draw from the source of love that we can sustain any kind of sacrificial love. Love is a natural outflow of Life. Just try to love someone who needs everything, gives nothing, never improves. It doesn't take long to lose patience. Kindness and endurance ebb away. The constant need for affection and affirmation becomes evident.

Ask the Lord why His love does not flow to others. *"What is the cause, Lord?"* The Spirit desires to remove the block, the root of the problem. Have you ever tried to "be kind?" God once said to me, "Be kind." Naively I thought the task would be easy. Well, yes, it was easy to be kind to the dogs, especially when they behaved. I was nice to people who liked me. I spoke kind words to strangers and to those whom I was trying to impress. It was difficult to love those who were unkind, rude, and insensitive. God kept showing me my sinful nature, my self-centeredness and my human needs. He showed me that I was much like the ones I criticized. I failed often; I was forgiven over and over again for my unkindness. My confession and repentance, and His forgiveness, released kindness. *"Those who have been forgiven the most, love the most."* (Lk.7:47)

His love is not discriminatory.
Jesus saw the real person. He was at home anywhere, with anyone. No one was worthless; no one was preferred due to status. Children, women, the demented, tax-collectors, the rich, the Pharisees, soldiers, the wretched, the wicked, the dirty, the unwashed were of equal importance. He touched them all with Life. He loved them as He was loved by the Father. Competition, comparisons, territorial disputes do not exist within the God-head. God's love embraces everyone.

How do I approach others? Do I use people to meet my needs? Do I cower in fear and inferiority? Do I intimidate others? Do I hide my real feelings? In each case, people are judged; a comparison of their worth and value is made. The question is, "How do I measure up to them?" My concern is about me, not the other person. Enter the human race and accept your status. You are neither better nor worse than others. We all are human, and therefore tragic as well as heroic, bad as well as good, interesting as well as boring, loving as well as hateful. Stop the comparisons! Jesus commands, "Get out of your chair! Come, wash feet!" It is only as we look beyond the expensive shoes or the filth of bare feet that we see with His eyes.

Jesus was intimately acquainted with His disciples and His other friends. He was with them day after day. It is important that we too have deep long-term relationships. So often in our culture, we are extremely busy. Gone are the days of visiting with friends and neighbors. This should not be, for it is here that we learn to love one another. We have turned over to the experts the caring for others. We advise, "A counselor can help you; a doctor would give medicine; a minister would comfort you." Are you friend to anyone, at all?

His Love sees the other person.
It is possible to be with people and never see them. I can say, "Hi, how are you?" and never hear the response. This should not be. Each moment with someone is an opportunity to love and touch him(her) with His love. "Hi, how are you?" can be that touch of care and love. The response is often, "Oh, just fine." Then he or she may divert the eyes and put up an invisible shield. If gently asked again, "How are you really?" He (she) shyly smiles, then tears up and reaches out. In that moment of time Love is exchanged. A light touch on the arm, says "I see you and care about you."

It is possible to live with children and a marriage partner and never know them. The words exchanged with each other are often either short choppy demands or perfunctory greetings. Oh please! This is not how it should be. The model the Son gave to us is one of knowing others. He knew Peter and his ways; He knew Martha and her serving; He knew Judas and his thievery. He took the time to find out what people wanted and the motives behind their requests. He confronted those who tried to touch him secretly because He wanted them to know Him, not just His power. Home is the place where all of our behavior is known. Do those who live with you know the Lord's love as He flows from you? Oh, I hope so.

Go to the grocery store and watch. Do you see poor, old sick Harry trying to find the soup? Do you speak a kind word then help him? Do you see the frustration of a young mother with three boys fighting over the cart? Do you pray for her? Observe the harried, stressed, handsomely dressed women dashing here and there in a great hurry. Do you smile and speak a simple greeting? These are opportunities to touch someone with gentle care and love. The Spirit longs to do so.

"Oh God, open my eyes and my heart."

His Love hears the cry of the human heart.
Love has a language all its own. Did you ever wonder how Jesus knew of events before they happened? He knew men before they disclosed anything. I believe this came about because He knew how to listen to the Father who gave Him perfect wisdom.

As we grow in our experience of listening to God, we then will have more wisdom to share with others. If I listen to others with a heart attuned to God, I hear much. Sometimes I hear joy, gladness, life. At other times I hear weariness, oppression, stress, fear, insecurity, and struggle. If I sincerely want to love this person, I can gently open communication by saying, "You seem so weary. It must be hard." This approach usually opens a conversation, communion, and love. The Father's voice within guides, *"Be gentle, be patient. Offer no solution. Let him find the way."* Others touch the Lord's love and wisdom as they touch me.

Paul writes, "Rejoice with those who rejoice, and weep with those who weep." (Rom.12:15)   Do you notice when someone is weeping without tears?   The language of love hears and knows, and then, loves and weeps with that person. Can you sense when someone is rejoicing? Do you give them ample space to share their good news? Can you put aside your opinions and listen and rejoice? Love hears the beloved. Love hears the Lord also.

His Love is passionate.
Several years ago people would describe me as gentle and quiet, right and proper, and somewhat joyful, though not passionate. I served my family, listened to them, drove them places, showed affection, yet I loved without vigor. Emotionally I was toned down from my natural extroverted personality. Anger was not appropriate. Enthusiasm was not proper. Tears flowed very rarely. This was not God's idea; I had invented a behavior I thought to be Christian.

It was then that I made a very naive request, *"God, Show me your passion."* He granted that request by shattering my proper behavior. Everyone and everything in my life broke my emotional control. He gave me abounding love; then He dealt with every love that competed with Him. Over and over again I heard, *"Love the Lord with All your heart. You shall have no other God before me!"* He demanded that everything and everyone whom I held as valuable be relinquished to Him. He alone was to be the source of comfort, companionship, and delight. He was not gentle. I was placed into situations which caused incredible pain. I experienced sorrow, hate, anger, love, grief, betrayal, fear, joy, and freedom.

He said, *"Go toward the pain so that your heart will remain tender not bitter."* I cried, and wailed, and struggled. He again said, *"Go towards the fear to conquer it so that it does not capture you."* He said, *"Be angry and sin not. There is truth worth standing for."* He said, *"Express thanks, and love, and gentleness."* He said, *"Where did your exuberance go? Be demonstrative in joy. Dance, cry, hug, express delight."* He said, *"Hate sin; hate dishonesty; hate compromise."* He said, *"Do not be afraid to love passionately."*

I wept over and loved those He loved. Each of these requests was enabled by the Spirit. It was as if God Himself inhabited my inner core and would rise to do what had been asked. I was then able to obey. I then had more freedom. This process continues today, and I am sure, I have only begun to learn His way. It is an incredible privilege though a very painful one.

Do you yearn to love as He did? Ask to know His Passion. Ask to know Love incarnate. His Presence both kills and releases at the same time. His love is terrible; His love is awesome. Oh, that we might release His extravagant, prodigal, lavish, abounding Love.

His love rejoices in the truth.
No one can judge or criticize you if you only say the appropriate things, or if you say nothing. It is also easy to share as an expert. If you have a doctorate in any subject, few have the expertise to challenge your knowledge. We are taught very early to say the right thing, in the right place, in the right way. Those who do not learn this are shunned, scorned, and rejected.

God has a different plan; He commands, *"Speak the truth in love."*

Truth and love cannot be separated. Speak truth because you love. Love is specific. Truth is specific. Now put them together; speak specific truth to the beloved, a difficult task because, as we have learned, truth is often received negatively at first. Loss of relationship may result; the beloved may hate you. Jesus rejoices in the truth and never withholds it even when the beloved is resistive. Hopefully, the beloved loves the truth, and will receive what is of the Lord. Again wisdom comes from the Lord, therefore it is imperative to listen carefully before speaking. Listen to the beloved; listen to the Lord. Be slow to speak. Truth spoken in love brings change. Truth is the wisdom of God. Love is the environment in which truth can be received.

His Love is a commandment.
To love as Jesus loved is not an option. There is never a guarantee that you will be loved in return. The beloved might leave to curse and swear like Peter. You may be betrayed for money. The one whom you desire to reach with love may hide from you. Yet, His love ushers in Life; You will never be the same again nor will the one you touch. Change, although painful, is full of Life. His love imbues others with a restful peace and exuberant joy.

We do not love others automatically. It is a choice to kneel, to touch, to wash, and to dry tired, dirty feet. Our time, our ways, our rights, must be set aside to create space for God to act through us. Our friends will then be known and loved. The servant King who washed eleven men's feet, resides in us. He longs to love using our eyes, ears, hands, mind, emotions and personality. He is the model; we are the living testimony.

Get up out of your chair and release Him to love...
the ones who are pretentious, self assertive, prideful.
the ones who promise to never leave yet do.
the ones who abandon you because of fear.
the ones who betray for power and money.
the ones in the inner circle, even when one is a traitor.
the ones who are lost.
the ones who want to be the most important.
the ones who are young, old, simple, dirty, rich, or poor.
the ones who do not believe.
the ones who have no spiritual perception.
the ones who are unbelieving believers.
the ones we live with everyday.

For this reason I bow my knees to the Father of our Lord Jesus Christ, from whom the whole family in heaven and earth is named that He would grant you according to the riches of His glory, to be strengthened with might through His Spirit in the inner man, that Christ may dwell in your hearts through faith; that you, being rooted and grounded in love, may be able to comprehend with all the saints what is the width and length and depth and height, to know the love of Christ which passes knowledge; that you may be filled with all the fullness of God.
(Eph. 3:14-19)

BETRAYAL

"A woman came having an alabaster flask of very costly oil of spikenard. Then she broke the flask and poured it on His head. But there were some who were indignant... But Jesus said, "Let her alone....She has done what she could. She has come beforehand to anoint My body for burial."

Then Judas Iscariot went to the chief priests to betray Him to them. And when they heard it, they were glad, and promised to give him money. So he sought how he might conveniently betray Him." (Mk:14:3,10-11)

The pop can tossed from the car ahead of us rolled across the road and into the ditch. The empty can had lost its value and was discarded. Old Sam, riding his balloon-tired bike, would eventually come along, stab it with a stick, lift it up, and put it into a sack. The can would be crushed, melted, used again and discarded once more.

I'm afraid that people are discarded too, and often for much the same reason. Their usefulness diminishes, and then, they are dismissed, discarded. Maybe an old Sam comes by to salvage what is left. Many times, however, they lie, so to speak, on the side of the road through summer, fall, winter, spring for years, without anyone noticing the loss, the loneliness, the wreckage of betrayal.

However, Jesus the Life-giver is in the business of picking up these cast-aways and returning them to life. It is my hope that we, like Jesus, give Life, not death, to others.

This chapter portrays a raw view of our proclivity to betray. It is hard to think of ourselves as a Judas; however, as humans we too often discard others. This chapter is a reality check; it is not pleasant to see this truth. However, this truth may prevent any one of us from being a betrayer, a death-giver. On the other hand, if you have been betrayed and are still unforgiving and hostile, the Lord wishes you to be free. When betrayed, it is essential to turn to the Father, not away from Him. How to maintain emotional and spiritual freedom in the midst of betrayal will be discussed in the next chapter, "Captivity and Freedom."

Betrayal occurs in close relationships. Only those whom I love can betray me. Those outside the intimate circle of my relationships do not hold this destructive power. Love is wonderful: the love of parent and child, the love between man and woman, the love between comrades, the love between friends. We must give and receive intimate love. If I never love deeply, I wither and die emotionally. Also I will never receive love if I do not risk rejection. Betrayal is the failure of human love which can be fickle, filled with self ambition and highly traitorous. If a loved one turns from us, we are cut to the quick; life itself is removed. Betrayal destroys trust and wounds the inner-most core of the human soul.

* * *

Come with me to Bethany, the home of Lazarus, Martha and Mary. Jesus came here often to enjoy their company and to rest. The servant King, the disciples, Simon the Leper, the two sisters, and Lazarus gathered for supper two days before Passover. It is during this time that extravagant human love was given to the Lord, and it is here Judas decided to betray Jesus.

Mary loved Jesus. She was still amazed and incredulous over the recent resurrection of Lazarus. Oh how she loved this wonderful man. Mary had one precious gift for Jesus, a token of her deep appreciation. It was a beautiful delicate alabaster flask filled with expensive precious spikenard, a fragrant oil from India. She came to Jesus while he sat at dinner, broke the flask and poured the oil over His head. It ran down his beard, dripped onto his robe. She then knelt, poured the oil on His feet. Her tears mixed with the spikenard. Tenderly she dried His feet with her hair. Her pure, wonderful, and extravagant worship poured over Him. The fragrance of her love, the sweet smell of the nard, filled the house. (Jn.12:3) Jesus welcomed the anointing and her tears. He might have taken His hand, lifted her head and looked into her face. "Thank you, Mary, for your love."

Here in this tender scene the disciples, and Judas Iscariot in particular, unkindly and with disregard, criticized Mary sharply. "What a waste. Her only treasure squandered in this disgusting show of affection."

Jesus strongly rebuked them for their cruel, harsh, critical judgment, "Leave her alone! She alone has prepared my body for death." His wounded bleeding head would be covered with the oil of her sacrificial gift. His beard, when plucked out, would smell of her devotion. The robe, the prize of a gambling game, would retain the fragrance of love. The feet washed with tears were ready for the nails. "Thank you Mary, for the anointing — for the grave." Oh yes, she knew how to worship and love her Messiah. The sweet smell of the oil in her hair would remind her of Him.

Right after this special dinner Judas left, found the religious leaders, and asked, "What will you give me — to betray Jesus? Judas discarded the Messiah that night.

Jesus, a man of sorrows and acquainted with grief, wept over Judas. He knew first hand the suffering and pain of betrayal.

* * *

Why write a chapter on betrayal? Our culture is drowning in the wreckage of betrayal. Drowning correctly describes the stifling of Life, a suffocation, a loss of all that is needed to live. I have watched many become numb, give up, and then continue to do right things without zeal or passion. As a counselor I have seen the tears; I have heard the despair: single parents alone to raise the kids and earn the living, fathers who have lost their children, home, income, and wife, children still hurt and confused years after the divorce, adults who keep stepping into one relationship after another only to repeat the tragedy once again. So many, so

many, all with the same pain, all discarded by others.
No one sees them, and no one can take the agony away.

People are betrayed all the time: children are betrayed by parents, the married never touch or talk, the employee goes to work, does the job, returns home. What he says or does makes no difference to anyone. There was a time when he was pursued, sought out, admired, now no one even says hello. You too may be the one who is no longer wanted. Over night you become the enemy and are rejected. The wife and kids are glad to be rid of you. Or at work the management takes your idea, develops the plan, hires others, and gives you a pink slip.

Jesus died to birth the church, the body of Christ, a community of love, truth, intimacy and accountability. This virgin fellowship has been ripped and torn by human disloyalty and betrayal. Can it ever fulfill its destiny as a Life-giving community?

Can you and I love when betrayal is likely? How does one go through this extremely difficult passage without becoming like Judas? It is easy to hate the betrayer and overlook our own proclivity to betray. What is it in the human heart that brings anyone to the desperate act of betrayal? The betrayer usually is someone who has been discarded by another and is desperately in need of love himself.

We have a choice to be like Jesus the Life-giver or like Judas the death-giver. As you read this dark chapter learn to be a Life-giver. Disloyalty and betrayal are a result of separation from the Father.

* * *

Betrayal — Someone, once loved, is violated and discarded for something or someone else.

He sat in my office with his head in his hands and struggled to tell me his story —

"I will never forget that awful day... I had no warning.
The house was strangely quiet... a note lay on the table."

> *'When you find this note I will be gone. Do not try to find me. Our marriage is over! It has been years since I have had any feelings for you. You have your life, and*

135

now, I am going to have mine. I have the children; I hope you will never see them again. My lawyer will contact you to arrange a financial settlement. And yes, there is someone else.'

"I stared at the note. The hackles rose on the back of my neck. I felt in mortal danger and turned cold and clammy. I could not believe what I read. Every voice inside me screamed, *No! This is not happening!* The terror of it all crept into my mind. *What was she doing? I was losing everything because of her. The children not here to tuck into bed....Not here to put their little arms around my neck and give me sweet Daddy kisses. No! No! Never! I'll fight for them.* Oh God! The rage...I wanted to run and scream and do violence, but all I could do was sit immobilized, frozen in shock. I vomited. My soul ripped apart. Rampant suspicion flooded in. *Who was the adulterer who had taken my wife? How could that have gone on right in front of me? What a fool I had been.* I screamed inner vows, *I'll never let someone do this to me. No women will make a fool of me! I'll make her pay! God, how could this be happening?* My blood turned to icicles.

I still cannot love anyone. That part of me died the day of her betrayal."

* * *

Horror Of Betrayal — Where Life And Death Meet
Betrayal is the deepest pain anyone can face, a horror, a living nightmare. God alone can bring life out of this dreadful place. If the Lord is excluded, this destructive behavior causes the death of the betrayer, the betrayed, and the community. It is imperative to understand this evil human tendency in order to prevent it. However, it is not enjoyable to look honestly at the motives and attitudes that lead to betrayal. What causes betrayal? The trail is clear.

Betrayal — The Inability To Trust God For Provision
Judas wanted something from Jesus. It might have been power, influence, wealth, control. Jesus did not provide this. Disappointed and offended, Judas stood aloof and judged Jesus as a betrayer, a defrauder. Judas then betrayed Jesus for a bag of silver. Strangely enough, Judas would have had what he wanted if he had waited to see the plan of God. Instead he took things into his own hands

136

and became the greatest traitor of all.

The root of betrayal starts with a strong desire to possess something or someone.

The desire may be material: a home, job, car. It might be power, approval, or adventure. It could be an emotional longing for love, security or independence. It may be the very human need for a companion, a sexual partner, intimacy with another. The war between what is desired and what the Lord knows we need, is constant. Man's way is to grab for happiness. If our affections are on man, woman, job, and/or "things," betrayal is just around the corner. Lust increases when what is desired does not satisfy. Life is then like a merry-go-round. With each turn we reach for the ring and lose every time. Jesus said, "What will it profit a man to gain the whole world, and lose his own soul."

Before you think, *"I would never betray the Lord or anyone close to me,"* look carefully at your longings and affections, for in them are the seeds of betrayal. If anything or anyone is lusted after as the source of happiness, it is an idol. An idol will disappoint you. Happiness will elude you. It is absolutely essential to relinquish to the Lord every object of adoration. Why? The Lord must be first; then He gives the most important things: love, joy, peace, patience, kindness, goodness, faithfulness, gentleness, and self-control. (Gal. 5:22-23) All of these things are in ample supply hidden in Christ Jesus. When He is in residence within, and has preeminence, you will possess them all.

What purpose motivates your life? What do you want? How will you get it? Will you use power, control, deception, treachery to have that beloved thing? Do you expect people to fulfill your desires? When they fail to meet that expectation, do you then consider them useless? Are they discarded like an empty can? Do you then go on to someone else?

Do you trust only God to meet your needs?

Betrayal — The Absence Of The Fear Of God
Would you rob a bank right in front of God? Of course not, yet often we act as if He is not present. During the three years that Judas spent with Jesus he was stealing money from the common

funds; he was a thief. (Jn.12:6) He believed he could get away with thievery and betrayal. This was his fatal mistake.

Without the fear of God, it is easy to think, *"I can do whatever it takes to achieve my goal."* No means are ruled out if the promised reward is enticing enough. What is clearly wrong becomes an option and leads to evil with malice aforethought. God sees everything and holds us responsible. Do not miscalculate. It matters to God what you do. You will reap what you sow.

Do you fear the Lord?

Betrayal — The Attitude Of Pride
The first evidence of pride is *separation* from others. A betrayer's internal attitude is one of pride. Judas might have thought, *"I know what I am doing. What foolishness to let a woman wash your feet with tears. I thought this man would be a real leader, instead he collects all the riffraff. He was to be a mighty ruler; this man will never make the grade."* Judas separated himself from the community of the King for Judas was sure he was right.

The second evidence of pride is a *critical spirit*. The traitor criticized, "Why did she waste the precious oil? Jesus doesn't even care how much was squandered on Him. Why all the fuss? All this emotional hysterical nonsense is just a gushy display of religious fervor. Look at her, how stupid."

The proud person criticizes others. People are considered untrustworthy, stupid, ugly, awful, dumb, shameful, silly. The judgment is: "I am not as they are." Others who are mentally ill, different in custom, or come from another part of the country; all are the brunt of crude jokes. Nationalities are stereotyped: "all green people are stupid." (Green is a safe color, isn't it?) "All management is out to take my money." "All churches are a scam." "The police...the government...the woman...men...." Critical, backbiting gossip pours from the mouth of the arrogant.

The third evidence of pride is a *pretense of righteousness*. To the proud person it is important to appear moral, to be right. No one seems so righteous as the one who is hiding unrighteousness. "She could have sold the oil and given the money to the poor." Sounds good, however, Judas had no concern for the poor. Many appear holy. They do good things. The man who tenderly

138

adores his wife in public, may hold her in a prison of criticism and abuse in private. The wife is Mrs. Sweetness and Light in public, and a shrike at home. A shrike is a bird which impales its victim on a thorn and then tears it apart muscle by muscle. A shrike is a person who torments another until he/she is weakened and wounded, then offers the victim comfort. In this act the shrike actually destroys the other bit by bit. 1

Do you think you are better than others?
Do you criticize others?
Do you pretend to be Godly in order to look righteous?

Betrayal — The Presence Of Deception

"I know I am right," when I am absolutely wrong, is an apt description of deception. The first to be deceived is the betrayer. Judas actually believed that his cause was righteous, a good thing. His rationale might have been: "Jesus is a fraud and should be killed."

Good never comes out of evil, yet the betrayer thinks it will. If questioned about motive, he is sure to blame the victim who he feels should be disposed of with all expediency. The deceived betrayer gathers around him those who agree with his viewpoint. He tells half truths to convince others of his opinion. They reassure him, "Of course, you are right. It is evident that this is God's will. You have a right to take charge, the sooner the better." The betrayer feels no remorse. He hears no counter counsel. At this point there is little anyone can do to overcome his rationale. Those able to set the record straight are usually not told of the plot. All is done in darkness and secret. Within the deception everything appears wonderful. "It will all work out for good, you'll see." The evil intent is obvious to those outside the plot. (Jesus dies. The disciples suffer incredible torment. Judas dies. Satan wins.) Of course, that is not the end of the story.

Please note, it is never the will of God for anyone to do an unrighteous deed in order to achieve a good thing. The fruit of betrayal may not be evident, but be assured, that what was conceived by the flesh will bring forth a harvest of corruption and death. Satan, the master of deceit, destroys not only the betrayed but everyone involved, especially the betrayer. "Do not be deceived, God is not mocked; for whatever a man sows, that he will also reap." (Gal 6:7) *Are you deceptive?*

Betrayal — The Use of Treachery

Treachery is the premeditated use of evil to destroy another in order to achieve what seems most important, much more important than any person. Each step of treachery becomes more deadly. Satan loves this road and will devour all who travel this path.

Judas, hiding deception in his heart, obtained information about Jesus to pass on to the religious leaders. This broke the sacred trust of his companions.

Treachery occurs when a betrayer leaves a tender, open atmosphere of love to betray another in order to gain a personal advantage. To tattle-tale is a breach in confidentiality. It sounds like this: "You will never believe what I heard. She..." "Really it is none of my business, but you really should know..." "I'm concerned about what was said. He is speaking against you." "I know he was upset, but really he is a danger to the business." Others report to others at the expense of the victim. Close friendships are destroyed forever when there is no confidentiality.

Note: It is not a breach of confidentiality when a *victim* tells the story to gain personal help. This must be done to gain freedom from the deception. The victim must be protected. If you are an observer of abuse, it is important to report the incidents to those who have authority to do something about it. If the treachery is not known to the victim, please go with one or two others, and tell him/her what you see and know. Please be careful to report only proven and known facts. It is imperative that truth prevail. Pray for wisdom. Be careful. If you go to the perpetrator, remember it is not likely he/she will change. The danger then increases for the one abused.

Judas, the traitor did everything for personal gain. Not only did he dip into the money bag, he schemed to gain political advantage. He secretly cheered the Pharisees and scribes as they sought to destroy Jesus who threatened their little kingdoms, their domains of religious self-righteousness and pride. In reality, Judas was part of their treachery.

Manipulation occurs when someone is deceived by another to

140

accomplish a secret agenda for personal advantage. The victim is unaware of the destructive plan to undermine him. His expertise is disregarded; his words discounted. The perpetrator sets traps to ensnare and tempt the victim. Gossip, lies, and misinformation is shared with others. He/she is made to feel wrong, stupid, at fault, crazy, or just plain unlovable. This is premeditated evil to wear down the victim and cause him/her to make a mistake that justifies the betrayal. The betrayer is sure he is right. Those involved in the betrayal dare to proclaim, "This is the will of God!"

The Pharisees hoped that Jesus would make a mistake. Of course, none was forthcoming. Power was then used to destroy Jesus.

> Then the chief priests, the scribes, and the elders of the people assembled at the palace of the high priest, who was called Caiaphas, and plotted to take Jesus by trickery and kill Him. (Mt.26:3-4)

The betrayer often uses the power of an institution to destroy the individual in order to fortify his own position and dominion. An institution is any social organization: government, marriage, church, business, and social or service club.

The perpetrator threatens, "You must comply with my demands. You had better do what I say. I'll tolerate no insubordination. You are rebellious to even question my authority." As a counselor, I have heard it all. The threats and cruel demands range from required participation in perverse immoral sexual behavior to on-the-job slavery.

Treachery leads to more evil. All communication is scrambled. What has been said is denied or changed. Defrauding (promises made and not carried out), ridicule, lack of forthrightness become the milieu. Demands are made that cannot be met. The victim tries harder and harder to comply with the abuser's demands. The betrayer does not want obedience; he is hoping for insanity.

The one betrayed is desperate, separated from others, and terrified. Most of the time the victim feels guilty for doing something terribly wrong which he has not done. Then the treacherous betrayer offers comfort and fraudulent sympathy. The victim feels relief and comfort, when, in fact, the shrike is destroying him/her.

The betrayer waits for just the right time to kill. The betrayed dies, spiritually, emotionally, and sometimes physically. (The can is tossed from the window and rolls into the ditch, discarded, useless, no longer valued, betrayed.)

Do you use treachery to achieve your goal?

In case you believe this to be an extreme example, think for a moment. You may have left a marriage for a better partner. You may be an insecure manager who is interested only in production; who never knows his employees. Or you might be a mover and shaker on the upward swing of success who believes that any sacrifice is worth the payoff. You and I may be any one of these.

* * *

Judas dies —

> Judas, with a great multitude with swords and clubs, came
> from the chief priests and the scribes and the
> elders...went up to Jesus and said, "Rabbi, Rabbi!" and
> kissed Him. Then they laid their hands on Him and took
> Him. (Mk.14:43-46)

With the victim removed, Judas thought he was free to do whatever he wished. He miscalculated. He forgot Satan; he also forgot God.

Satan laughed —

The spirit of death overwhelmed Judas.

Then Judas, His betrayer, seeing that He (Jesus) had been condemned, was remorseful and brought back the thirty pieces of silver to the chief priests and elders, saying, "I have sinned by betraying innocent blood." And they said, "What is that to us? You see to it!" Then he threw down the pieces of silver in the temple and departed, and went and hanged himself. (Mt. 27:3-5)

* * *

Jesus gives Life — Jesus the Life-giver suffered the searing pain of betrayal. The servant King alone, distressed, oppressed by Satan's attack, abandoned by friends, cried in agony, "Let this pass! Not this cup! Father is there another way?" What was the Father's answer? We are not told. Jesus replied, "Not my will, but yours, Father!" (Lk.22:24) The Father was His source of Life. The Father's plan was before Him. It required His death. He relinquished power; He gave His Life. He was not a Judas.

* * *

When we are betrayed it is difficult to be like Jesus. Destruction is near at hand. Miscalculation and deception abound. Anger gives rise to a desire for revenge. Fear threatens to overwhelm reason. Everything we thought trustworthy shifts. The Lord is our only stability, and yet, He is often blamed for our misfortune. "This is not fair. God, why are You treating me like this?"

Satan laughs —

How can you remain free even when the situation is oppressive? How did Jesus stay free even when betrayed? The next chapter will answer these questions. I hope that none of you will become captive to bitterness and revenge. Satan desires the betrayed to be coupled with the betrayer, linked forever in hatred. You will then be suspicious, afraid, revengeful, a captive of the spirit of death. Your life will be consumed by death-giving. If however you turn to the Father in love, he will transform you into the image of His Beloved Son.

If you have found yourself face to face with betrayal, or looked into the mirror and found Judas, there is a way to end your misery. Alone, distressed, oppressed by Satan, abandoned by friends, betrayed, you must turn to the Father. Betrayal reveals what is in the heart. Will you be able to respond to betrayal as Jesus did, or will you sit alone, separated, and afraid? Jesus never left the Father. He chose the path of the Life-giver. Do you want to follow Him?

Oppression ends when —

You and I humbly cry out...

"Oh God, change the desires of my heart to be like yours."

"Help me honor your daily presence that keeps me from evil."

"Take away my pride so I value others."

"Help me to be straight forward."

"Let no dark secrets remain in me."

"Oh God, keep me from betrayal and treachery."

"I need your help."

"I will die here and not finish your assignment unless you have mercy on me."

You and I confess...

"Sometimes I am like Judas."

"I am traitorous at heart."

"I want my own way."

"Oh God, help me to be like you, Jesus."

You and I desire to continue...

"Oh, God, give me courage to continue."

"Help me to forgive."

"What a privilege to suffer in this place."

Let us lay aside every weight, and the sin which so easily ensnares us and let us run with endurance the race that is set before us, looking unto Jesus, the author and finisher of our faith, who for the joy that was set before Him endured the cross.. (Heb.12:1)

14

CAPTIVITY
AND FREEDOM

"Then they came and laid hands on Him and took Him..."(Mt.27:37)

Captivity and Freedom are opposites of each other. However, God can turn captivity into freedom even within very difficult circumstances. This chapter is written especially to you who are in painful injurious situations. How does God bring freedom to the desolate lonely captive?

Freedom
These vignettes portray different aspects of freedom.

I gently held the tiny wren in my hand. The little bird had hit the window, was stunned, but not seriously injured. I opened my hand; the wren fluffed its feathers and flew away. The word for this is manumit, to let go from the hand. 1 The bird was...
Free to re-enter life...

The farmer revved up the tractor, put it in gear and lowered the plow into the hard earth. The soil was turned over and loosened by the plow. The earth was...
Free to receive life...

I remember running through a field of wild daisies when I was about eight years old. Exuberant and filled with energy, I was...
Free to express life...

"There was a woman present, so twisted and bent over with arthritis that she couldn't even look up. She had been afflicted with this for eighteen years. When Jesus saw her, he called her over. "Woman, you're free!" He laid hands on her and suddenly she was standing straight and tall, giving glory to God." (Lk. 13:10-11) 2
She was...
Free to enjoy life...

He was addicted to pornography. All of his thoughts were filled with lust and sexual fantasy. There came a day when he was freed from bondage, forgiven, and washed clean inside and out by a loving Savior. He was...
Free to love...

Our golden retriever, with great anticipation, watched the trainer throw the stick into the water. The dog did not move for he was under command to *"stay and watch!"* On the command, *"Fetch!"* He tore down the bank, jumped into the creek, splashed through the water, and seized the stick. He returned it to the trainer who gave him great praise. He was...
Free to obey...

"King David danced before the Lord with all his might...So David and all the house of Israel brought up the ark of the Lord with shouting and with the sound of the trumpet." (2Sam.6:14-15)
The Biblical word 'rejoice' means to spin around before the Lord. David freely rejoiced before the Lord. Without shame he expressed great joy. He was...
Free to rejoice...

All of these illustrations depict different expressions of freedom. Each portrays a liberty, an unrestricted and freely made action.

Captivity
Captivity is the opposite of freedom. A captive is prevented, constrained, unable to move at will, to think for himself, to choose an action and then perform it. Emotions are locked within or are inappropriate due to bitterness, anger, hatred, or fear.
I watched a spider and a fly. At first, the fly was caught by only

146

one wing. With a little help from the wind, it looked as if he would be free from the web. However, each time he tried to free himself the movement of the web attracted the attention of the spider who quickly descended from his hiding place to wrap another strand around the buzzing unfortunate. The fly, captive in the web, was soon eaten for dinner. We sometimes feel like the fly. Caught in imprisoning circumstances, we find escape almost impossible.

Captivity and Freedom
The Old Testament story of Daniel in the lion's den is a tale of both captivity and freedom. Darius, a heathen king, had issued a command. His subjects were to pray only to him. Disregarding the king's edict, Daniel continued to pray to God. As a punishment for disobedience, he was tossed into a pit with the lions. Imagine the scene: the lions roaring, the envious schemers glad to be rid of their competition, a wishy-washy king wringing his hands, and faithful Daniel soon to die, destined for the same fate as the fly. God intervened. The black fearsome pit was suddenly filled with light from the angel of the Lord. The lions were strangely quiet as the angel might have greeted each with a pat on the head, *"Hello, how are you?"* Daniel was forgotten. Can you hear Daniel's shouts of joy and see him dance like David? (Of course, although we do not know these details, it is fun to imagine how it might have been, isn't it?) We do know that Daniel saw God turn captivity into freedom. (Dan. 6:10-23)

Fortunately, our destiny is not that of a fly caught in the web. Maybe we are in circumstances as hopeless as Daniel's. We may have been betrayed and discarded, abused and persecuted, or just plain ignored and disregarded. People and events hold us captive. God longs to turn that captivity into freedom, to bring hope and deliverance, to bring Life.

You will remain bitter and lonely, filled with hatred and pain unless you turn to God in the midst of misery. The Father is the only source of Life. He may leave you in the circumstance and give you Life right there. On the other hand, He may make a way of escape and greet you outside the prison. Liberty is possible in any circumstance. Jesus remained free even after Judas initiated a betrayal that led to physical captivity.

* * *

147

The Desolate Place

On the night of His betrayal, alone and desolate, Jesus saw the horror of His immediate future. Was there no way of escape? He had poured Life from the Father to the people, yet they were not free from the bitterness of human suffering. Unaware of his sorrow and struggle, his friends would all abandon him. He asked them to watch and stay close, but they slept. There was no comfort. Oppressed, crushed with grief, Jesus cried in anguish of soul. Was there anything else he could do?

You may have been in a lonely, desolate place, also. You may be there now. Jesus, the man, a very human man, understands the pain.

Jesus did not want to be falsely accused, ridiculed, tortured, and then slaughtered as a sin offering. Here in the garden, the desolate place, He despaired, "*I know that the Father will not save me. I will be like forsaken, ravaged Jerusalem when her enemies plundered and destroyed her. I can still hear the scream of the children, the wail of the starved, the howl of the jackals, the triumphant shouts of the victors. The enemies of God will kill me. Death will enjoy this victory. It begins. Is there any other way to bring Life to the dying Earth? Must the living seed be placed into the ground to die? Father, it is time. Keep my friends from the evil one.*" There was no comfort, no reprieve. The sweat poured from his body like great drops of blood falling to the ground as He relinquished everything to the Father.

The Father

The Father heard his anguish, knew His struggle. God did not deliver Him for He saw the finished work, as did the Son. Instead the Father gave Jesus the gift of endurance. Strengthened, Jesus prayed, "*Father I gave them your word; You were fully present as I did your work. I yearn for them to love as we do; they will be the habitation of God, your holy temple. May they have my peace and joy. May they know perfect wholeness (holiness). Sin, disease, death fill the Earth. I will soon gather these into myself, so that when I am sacrificed (slaughtered), their power will be broken.*" The Father listened to His only begotten Son whom He loved.

Inner Communion

Jesus gave the Father his agony; the Father ushered the Son into the light-filled, quiet, peaceful, inner spiritual place without dimension, without time, without limit. The Father alone occupied this holy place. Jesus listened to the voice of God, *Kol Yahweh,* the voice of His Father. This beloved Life-filled Voice is Love, Wisdom, Perception. Jesus, the Incarnate Word, and the Father shared together the sorrow and the joy of the coming events. Then Jesus embraced His Father's will. *"I must complete the task as Life-giver."*

Obedience To The Voice Of The Father

Jesus had lived His life on earth guided by the Voice of the Father. The powerful and creative Word of God flowed into the world from the Father through Jesus. It was as if Jesus had an open door within tuned to the deep inner power of that loving Voice. As Jesus experienced each day and encountered human misery and death, the Father gave Him Life to share. Jesus listened to the outer world at the same time His Spirit heard His Father. Therefore, He was then able to discern the intent of those who came to Him. He heard what they did not say; He knew their thoughts. He knew the secret desires of those afraid to approach Him, unlike the boisterous who loudly stated their needs. He heard the desperate: the prostitutes, the leprous, the demon possessed, the poor as they cried for mercy. He discerned the intent of the religious leaders; a few really did want to know Him. He knew each person and their needs. As He listened within to the voice of the Father, the Word of God flowed from Him to bring Life to these living dead.

Always He had lived in the great strength of the Father's voice. Now that voice would accompany Him in death. He was free from fear for He did what the Father commanded. Man could kill only the body. Jesus had decided long, long ago to give His life. He would return to the Father with His last agonized whisper, *"Father, into thy hands I commend my Spirit,"*

* * *

Our Desolate Place

Feelings of isolation and loneliness haunt most of us much of the time. It seems that the very fabric of social order is disintegrating. Everywhere people feel isolated and forsaken, *"No one cares, no one sees me, no one knows me!"* Betrayal is all around, in every job, in every relationship, in every home. Most of us have few close friends. Gone are the days of enduring friendships. Families move frequently; jobs change often. Kids move from school to school; Christians roam from church to church. People try harder and harder to have good marriages, to be good parents. The effort brings increasing fatigue, weariness, and stress. Many do not even know what it is that they are longing to find.

This experience of isolation and numbing inner pain I have chosen to call the desolate place. The Hebrew root word for desolate, *shamem,* means to stun, or grow numb. *3* Revival must come to you and me in this lonely place. Somehow, we must return to life. Unfortunately, when someone is almost spiritually and emotionally dead, it is impossible for him/her to do anything. What is it then that brings revival?

The numbness, the desolation must be recognized. Many of us try to relieve the symptoms of loneliness by changing surface circumstances. However, the loneliness continues even if people, jobs, churches, hobbies, vacations and physical location are rearranged. It will not help to hang on a little longer. Do not think that God will just take care of things automatically. Do not hope the wife/husband will change, and then it will be better. Do not wait for the boss to be kind and appreciative. Do not look for that perfect person, that perfect union, the excitement of a new affair, a lover who will seek you out to embrace you. The change might bring relief for a time. However, the isolation will return. These things will not make any permanent difference.

When you admit your misery, your desolation will become evident. You will then experience anger and rage; the hurt and hatred will ooze out; hope will vanish. Go to a private quiet place and ask the Lord what is wrong. Speak to Him about your frustration and pain, your love and hate, your disappointment, confusion. Confess your regrets, your shame, your fear. Put everything on the table. He can handle your anger, your cries and groans, your tears and wretchedness. Usually there is an intense urge to flee back into noise, busyness, people, addiction, or sleep. Do not do that; sleep if you must, then begin again. Unless you are entirely honest with yourself and God, nothing will change. You will remain numb and almost dead. However, if you sincerely want to find the deep root of your despair, God will meet you. His answer is usually different than expected.

Hope can die quietly, a little at a time. In this desolate place, hope that has long been buried, surfaces. It is devastating to see the disparity between hope and reality. Discouraged and disappointed, most of us will scream, *"Oh no! How did this happen?"*

It is here that you must decide to turn to the Father. Sadly enough, it is often hard to trust God. Deep inside you may harbor a resentment towards Him. *"Isn't He ultimately to blame for this? How did He let it happen? Is He evil or good? Is He in control of everything or not?"* These are hard, hard questions when life has been brutally unfair.

The Father hates sin. He did not cause it. People make choices independently from Him and often their choices are both self-serving and injurious to others.

I am writing to a number of my friends who feel alone, whether living with people or by themselves. Each of you feel no one understands, cares, or can help. You cannot give up, yet you have no energy to continue. I speak to you; I want you to find the Father.

If you do not relate to this place of despair, please be patient with those who do. You may indeed be happy. Do not try to dig up some despair that is not there. Enjoy your life. Be thankful. At some future time you may need to remember these lessons. If you learn the process, you may be able to help a despairing friend find the Lord.

When someone is desperate many inner voices compete for attention. One voice is that of escape, *"You have to do something, anything to stop the pain."* Another voice condemns, *"You must have done something wrong. If you were worth loving someone surely would love you."* Another discourages, *"You have tried everything only to come back to this! You cannot win."* Other words urge more effort, *"Just read the Bible; pray."* Unbelief weaves its deadly theme into this milieu, *"God is not real. You have imagined a fantasy creature. Give it all up."* Then the opposite arguments come, *"No, I know God is real. No, there must be a way."*

Place all of it, everything — the present situation, all your feelings, disappointments, doubts, unbelief before the Lord. Place those who have carved you up and spit you out before the Lord. Wait! This is called relinquishment. Many of the Psalms express this posture.

> The secret of the Lord is with those who fear Him, and He will show them His covenant. My eyes are ever toward the Lord, for He shall pluck my feet out of the net. Turn Yourself to me, and have mercy on me, for I am desolate and afflicted. The troubles of my heart have enlarged; bring me out of my distresses! Look on my affliction and my pain, and forgive all my sins. Consider my enemies, for they are many; and they hate me with cruel hatred. Keep my soul, and deliver me; Let me not be ashamed, for I put my trust in You. Let integrity and uprightness preserve me, for I wait for You. (Ps.25: 15-21)

The cry from the desolate place is always heard by the Father. He knows the agony, the anguish.

Turn To The Father
The Father comes to the forsaken. He knows what to do and how to do it. His first step is to strengthen the desperate with the gift of endurance. Sometimes we would rather die than to go on struggling. However, He does not want our death. He wants us to live. At first nothing seems to get better. Actually, to tell you the truth, things will seem worse. The pain is excruciating, the emotions raw, the agony acute. God did not numb the pain for Jesus either; He knew intense suffering.

Why experience the pain? Even if you do not feel emotional pain the cause of the despair is still there. The pain will appear in disguise all the time. How is your temper when you drive? Does it show in the way you play racquetball or golf? Is it absolutely essential for you to win every argument? Anger seeps out in cutting words, curses and oaths, rudeness, self-pity. You may often demand and control, manipulate and ridicule. On the other hand, you may remain silent, not venturing out of your dark angry self-pity. You might just sit and watch television, blanked out, aware of no one. You alone know how the hidden despair slithers out to wound others. If the truth be known, you can no longer control

152

your behavior. Umm...sounds like you have become like those you despise. I hope not. Place all before the Father, and He will sort out the rubbish.

Inner Communion

God's voice is present beneath all the others. Listen...His is a steady, insistent, quiet voice, truthful, loving, filled with mercy. His voice comes from deep within for He resides in you.

God speaks clearly. His Word is neither vague, hard to discern, nor difficult to obey. He will get the message to you if you listen to Him in the midst of all the competition. However, you must *"shut up and sit down."* If you prefer, *"Be quiet, settle down, and listen!"* I'm sure you have spoken these words hundreds of times. Follow your own advice. Another way to say this is, *"At—-ten—-tion!"* It is imperative for you to recognize His Voice in order to enjoy his Presence.

His Word contains power. He speaks specifically to you of his merciful forgiveness. The truth is uncovered. His encouragement lifts the darkness. Perception changes. You no longer see the splinter in your neighbor's eye, but the log is yours. Most of all He speaks of His love. Many times, however, when He touches us with Love, we reject it. *"No one could love me."* *"God doesn't care about me."* *"I'm a nobody going nowhere."* Yes, He has heard all of that before. It does not matter. He can only love.

One night during a lonely hike the Lord spoke to me. *"When you walk with others I choose to join you. When you go alone you choose to walk with me. I love these walks; I love to love you, play with you, sing with you, direct you, teach you."* With these words my attitude changed. Think of it, a God who loves to be with me. Hard to imagine, yet, how true!

The Father meets us any place, anywhere. There is also another place He longs to show us. I wrote of this spiritual experience in my journal:

> This spiritual place is without dimension or time. It is full of the very Life of the Father, light-filled, quiet, peaceful. It is here we know that He is faithful. It is here we know we are sinful yet forgiven. It is here we know direction and

153

purpose. It is here we are healed. This place is in our spirit. The Father gently brings us into a large, new wondrous knowledge of Him. Wisdom from the Father moves into the mind. Lovingkindness surrounds the broken-heart. The stony places in the soul break up and soften, ready for new life. His hand holds us until we can once again fly. The internal deception breaks away. We then see our sin; we see the enemy as God sees him. We can feel the warmth of His joy emerge through all the tears, disappointment, and loneliness. His glory lights the sterile coldness of our isolation. We no longer feel desolate, alone. He warms us. Gently He speaks comfort. He gives us courage to open the door once again and welcome others.

This quietness, this awareness of His presence within, can go into the world. We can learn to quiet down inside and immediately access His direction and guidance. We have an open door to the Father all the time. If you do not have this communion, ask the Lord to draw you into His presence. The constant awareness of God is not automatic. He has not abandoned you.
Cry out, "Daddy, Daddy, God." (Abba, Abba Father)

Loneliness is a sign that we miss the Father.

Obedient To The Voice Of God
"...though Jesus was a Son, yet He learned obedience by the things which He suffered." (Heb.5:8) The Word of God, both written and spoken, the Voice of God is the standard and the directive. When we can hear the Lord, He gives us the power to change. He provides everything needed. Obedience is not the carrying out of a set of orders, rules, regulations. Obedience is perfect freedom. We need only to open the inner door of our spirit and listen.

The Word is straightforward. *"Be still." "Observe! What do you see?" "Listen, what do you hear? Now, what do you know?" "Speak the truth. Do not be afraid." "Be gentle with him, he is discouraged." "Don't cover your pain, stay open so others may help."* Each situation is different. Sometimes we need to repent. He shows us the root of our disobedience. At other times we might want to flee a situation; the Lord commands us to stay and watch His hand move on our behalf. The inner voice of God is

154

never in conflict with the written word of God. His Word makes sense immediately. We may not understand its complete implications, but what we do understand is always clear.

To be obedient to God, we must be absolutely dependent upon Him. When the Word of God is divorced from the living person of God, it kills. It leads to striving. If however, guidance is learned from the hand of the Lord, little by little we live by His Spirit.

Seek the Lord with your whole heart. Seek the Lord —- *Seek the Lord* —- **Seek the Lord**, not ways of escape, easy solutions, appeasement, or prescribed methods. Learn to live in His presence. Desire and love the solitude of the quiet place. You then will know what is right, true and good.

The path out of the desolate place leads to one place. Your life, your flesh, must manifest His Life. Jesus' life must radiate from you. Your life is to be conformed to the image of the Son. You then will give Life; you will love passionately; you will suffer as He did. God is the source of whatever you need. All, everything that you need to give to others is yours.

You can live this way only if you constantly return to the Father. Over and over again we become depleted, desolate. It is time, once again to put everything on the table, to admit the frustration, and to relinquish everything again to the Lord. The Father listens and draws us into the quietness so that we hear His voice. His wondrous Voice, His Word replenishes us again with His Life. Freedom is ours when we are obedient. When in captivity, no matter what the circumstance, embrace the desolate place, for it is here that revival first comes.

* * *

God draws each of us into this path to freedom. You are not alone. If you find a companion, a counselor, a pastor who can come along with you into the lonely desolate place, you are indeed fortunate. However, the process does not change. No one else can deal with your pain. Someone else can strengthen you, add discernment, and of course, pray. Your friend must give your suffering dignity. To offer suggestions, quick solutions, or methods of healing dishonors you. It is very helpful if he/she is just present.

155

If you are the friend, please, *be* there. Do not try to get your friend fixed so you can get on with your own life. If you promise to see your friend through this incredibly painful and difficult time, do not break your promise. Any disloyalty on your part will add to the burden. If you do not know how to walk with someone without anxiously hurrying the process, step back. Wait for the Lord's instructions. Read this chapter again. Your friend must find the Lord. God alone is the source of Life. Both of you must find Life in the midst of the pain.

Remember we learn His way as we live. The lessons are not necessarily sequential. Life contains opportunities to choose to listen and learn as we are God-tuned. We can remain free only as we know God. He is the only security, the source of everything, even when life turns upside down.

> We have this treasure in earthen vessels, that the excellence of the power may be of God and not of us. We are hard-pressed on every side, yet not crushed; we are perplexed, but not in despair; persecuted, but not forsaken; struck down, but not destroyed— always carrying about the body of the dying of the Lord Jesus, that the life of Jesus also may be manifested in our body. For we who live are always delivered to death for Jesus' sake, that the life of Jesus also may be manifested in our mortal flesh. (IICor. 4:7-11)

> We carry this precious Message around in the unadorned clay pots of our ordinary lives. That's to prevent anyone from confusing God's incomparable power with us. As it is, there's not much chance of that. You know for yourselves that we're not much to look at. We've been surrounded and battered by troubles, but we're not demoralized; we're not sure what to do, but we know that God knows what to do; we've been spiritually terrorized, but God hasn't left our side; we've been thrown down, but we haven't broken. What they did to Jesus, they do to us — trial and torture, mockery and murder; what Jesus did among them, he does in us — he lives! Our lives are at constant risk for Jesus' sake, which makes Jesus' life all the more evident in us." (II Cor. 4:7-11) 4

15

ACCUSATION

The high priest said to Him, "I put You under oath by the living God: Tell us if You are the Christ, the Son of God!" And Jesus said to him, "It is as you said. Nevertheless, I say to you, hereafter you will see the Son of Man sitting at the right hand of the Power, and coming on the clouds of heaven."

Then the high priest tore his clothes, saying, "He has spoken blasphemy!...He is deserving of death." (Mt. 26:59-68)

They put up over His head **The Accusation** *written against Him: This Is Jesus The King Of The Jews.*
(Mt. 27:37)

Do you and I make false assumptions that lead to erroneous accusations? Unfortunately we often do. Our eyes and ears deceive us. It is difficult for two of us to agree on the simplest matters. Our conversations may be like this, "Did you see her smile?" "It wasn't a smile, she was squinting." "You said this!" "No I didn't. I said..." Jesus had a different way of making judgments. We learn from Him a new way to evaluate others and ourselves. We learn how to face false accusation. We learn to be careful when judging others.

* * *

The Jewish leaders accused Jesus of every kind of mischief. Their accusations began when He healed and forgave a paralyzed man. The Pharisees charged, "No one can forgive sin except God. You are guilty of blasphemy!" They thought Jesus was just a carpenter from Nazareth, Mary's son, a common working man, an illegitimate child. "Jesus Messiah, hog wash!" At another time Jesus healed a crippled man on the Sabbath. The religious leaders cried, "Sabbath breaker, law breaker." They murmured, "Look at the company He keeps. He drinks too much wine and stuffs himself with food." "He doesn't even wash before meals." "He must be a Samaritan." "He is crazy, a demon possessed sinner, a liar."

The religious leaders looked askance as the people followed Him. "First thing you know the whole Hebrew nation will be perverted. The people, already stirred up, misled, will rebel against Caesar. Jesus won't listen to any of us, the elders, the scribes, the Pharisees. He openly dishonors us before the people. He is not Messiah! He should die for this deception, lawlessness, rebellion, demon worship, and blasphemy." Jesus was innocent!

* * *

How Jesus Faced Accusation
Jesus responded to the Father, not to the accusers.
Jesus always listened to the Father who gave Him wisdom in every situation. Sometimes Jesus answered the criticism with a story. At other times He walked through the crowd and left His accusers in the dust. His mission as Life-giver was His priority.

Jesus knew the truth.
He was Messiah, God's Son. Because Jesus was certain of His mission as Life-giver no one could intimidate Him. He challenged His opponents for their false logic and hypocritical accusations. "If you knew my Father, you would know me!" (Jn.8:42) You do not know the Father, and therefore you err!"

Jesus discerned the intent of the accuser.
He forthrightly spoke to the arrogant Scribes and Pharisees. Read

Matthew chapter twenty-three. You can sense his anger and offense against the religious leaders.

> You do everything to be seen by men. For a pretense you make long prayers. Blind guides, fools! You neglect the weightier matters of law: justice and mercy and faith. You strain out a gnat and swallow a camel! For you cleanse the outside of the cup and dish, but inside they are full of extortion and self indulgence. You are like white-washed tombs which indeed appear beautiful outwardly, but inside are full of dead men's bones and all uncleanness. Even so you also outwardly appear righteous to men, but inside you are full of hypocrisy and lawlessness. Serpents, brood of vipers! You murder and persecute the prophets. (Summary: Mt.23, author's paraphrase)

Jesus spoke the truth.
He never compromised the truth to protect Himself. He did not answer the trumped up charges brought in His trial. However, when asked, "Are you the Christ?" He answered, "It is as you say." When Pilate asked, "Are you King of the Jews?" He answered, "You tell me. Because I am King, I was born and entered the world so that I could witness to the truth. Everyone who cares for truth, who has any feeling for the truth, recognized my voice." (Jn.18:37) 1

* * *

How Is Our Discernment?
Do we judge others based on our own thoughts? Are we like the religious leaders? Do we totally miss God as we go through life? I would like you to observe a small group of Christians as they utterly fail to see as God sees, love as God loves. Learn from this horrid example. God forbid that we might be just like the Pharisees, like these sisters.

> This little group meets once a week for Bible study and prayer. Today one of the group, lets call her Heather, disturbed and desperate, shares: "Nothing seems to help. I wake up at night soaking wet, then I can't sleep. My head is pounding. My back aches. I get up and wander around the house. I look into the refrigerator.

159

I think, '*Maybe some warm milk will help.*' I heat it up, take a sip and immediately get nauseated. '*What is wrong with me?*' '*What have I done to deserve this?*' I pray and pray; God doesn't seem to listen. This has gone on for months. I know that all of you are tired of my complaints. At home I can't get anything done. The house is a wreck; the dishes pile up. I'm lucky if I can warm up a can of soup for dinner. My poor husband tries to help. At first he was patient. Now He gives me lists, goals, little lectures. He gets mad; he sulks. I am getting worse not better." She sits and sobs.

The others stir; some are impatient; some give advice; some say nothing; some want her to stop her emotional outburst.

"Heather, have you tried vitamins? Your diet is not what it should be. My aunt stopped eating tomatoes and miraculously got over her headaches."

"Honey, I've watched and listened to you for several months now. I've prayed for you for years. God has put this on my heart. If you had more faith, God would hear your prayers and heal you. Claim the promises of God. You know that He gives us great and precious promises, but we must claim them, stand on the word. When you complain, you allow unbelief to rob you of faith. 'Lord, help Heather stand fast on Your Word. I rebuke her unbelief. And Lord, if there is any hidden sin in her life, help her confess it. Deliver her!' "

Heather looks up and says, "I am weak in faith, but really this doesn't help. I've heard all of this before. I try and try to do what all of you say. It doesn't work. I'm beginning to doubt the value of prayer. Nothing happens when I pray. Maybe God is up there somewhere, but He has not been in my house lately. He is like a fair weather friend, when you feel good, he seems to be present. You people are like that too. I've come here for help, and all you do is judge me. You should be kind to a sick friend. Instead you accuse me without the slightest fear of God. It is wonderful for you to speak truth, but your criticisms arc not based on fact."

"Now just listen here. We have been extremely patient with all your complaints. Don't go accusing us of lack of concern. What you need to do is just buck up. Take a shower, get outside and exercise. Sing praise songs. Stop drinking coffee. No wonder you can't sleep. Confess all this resentment and unbelief to the Lord. Then He might answer your prayer."

"I know I'm not perfect. Who is? You, however, think you know everything. Because I just don't get better, you give me more and more advise. I can't bear it anymore. Just leave me alone."

"Now, now dear. We really are concerned. There must be something you need to change. You seem angry with your husband? Complaining about him dishonors him."

"What does that have to do with how I feel?
I'm going home."

"We'll pray for you, honey. You know that we love you. Maybe a little rest. Have you had a good physical lately? Oh yes, I remember you went to the doctor, and he found nothing. Sounds to me like a good counselor might be a help.

Heather stumbles out of the meeting.

The others go on without her.
"Lord, I just don't know what is wrong with her. She used to be such a sweet girl. She shouldn't talk in such a disrespectful manner about You and her husband. Lord, break her deception. Keep her under your judgment until she learns what you want her to know."

"If she is not a Christian, Lord save her. Sometimes I discern a strong independent spirit. It may be pride. We come against it. Help her poor husband to rise up and take the leadership in the home. If he were a spiritual man, this probably would not have happened. He has left her uncovered, and the enemy has come in to torment her."

161

The meeting comes to an end.

At home Heather cries. "What is wrong. No one understands. I'm not making this up? I've done everything I know to do? Every day I feel worse. Maybe I'm crazy. My back is worse; I can't eat anything; I'm dizzy. God...I need your mercy."

Heather's husband comes home from work to find his wife strangely still. He calls. She does not stir. She had died of a ruptured brain aneurysm several hours earlier.

No one took the time to gather correct information, to believe her story, to support her in the pain, to find a solution. She died alone; unloved. She returned to the loving merciful Father.

* * *

Jesus present in the meeting to comfort, to heal, to assist, to uphold and to strengthen was not consulted. The spirit of man gave Him no invitation. He was not permitted to heal for the arrogant already knew the answers.

Presumption is extremely difficult to face. Regretfully, I have been part of the pompous crowd. I thought I had all the answers, thought I knew, thought I understood. I have prayed those prayers and have injured others.

I also have been like Heather. I had needs and pain that just didn't go away. Others gave advice, patted me on the head, and took pity on me. Some jumped to conclusions, blaming and condemning my husband. Often no one really listened.

Dear readers, we often miss the Christ for we never wait long enough to hear His wisdom before we express our own opinion.

Fortunately at other times, I have experienced Jesus as He flowed through others, incarnate in them. His magnificent love tenderly and wondrously touched me through ordinary human vessels. When we walk closely with the Lord He is able to bring love and comfort through us. It would be nice if this occurred all the time. It does not. Sometimes we minister Life and hit the mark, at other times, we sadly miss. Unfortunately, there is always a mixture.

Some of you may recognize Heather's story. It is in the Bible. Job and his friends said much the same things. Read the book of Job; read a lesson of human presumption.

* * *

The Spirit Of God Invited To Judge
How did Jesus judge others? How did He see others? Isaiah chapter eleven gives us insight into how Jesus judged:

> There shall come forth a Rod from the stem of Jesse,
> And a Branch shall grow out of his roots.
> The Spirit of the LORD shall rest upon Him,
> The Spirit of wisdom and understanding,
> The Spirit of counsel and might,
> The Spirit of knowledge and of the fear of the LORD.
> His delight is in the fear of the LORD,
> And He shall not judge by the sight of His eyes,
> Nor decide by the hearing of His ears;
> But with righteousness He shall judge the poor,
> And decide with equity for the meek of the earth;
> He shall strike the earth with the rod of His mouth,
> And with the breath of His lips He shall slay the wicked.
> Righteousness shall be the belt of His loins,
> And faithfulness the belt of His waist.

Jesus cut off the old religious vine with its complex system of rules. Instead He judged by the Spirit of God Who rested upon Him. This word *rest* in the Hebrew describes an atmosphere of steadiness, quiet, security, stillness, and peace. This also describes the quiet place of the Father. Jesus lived in settled quiet security. As a result He knew the Voice of God as the Word flowed into His spirit. His reverence for the Father and the Spirit constantly under-girded Him. Acutely aware of the Father, He was filled with delight.

He spoke wisdom, understanding, and counsel by the power of God. The Spirit of all knowledge surrounded Him. His human

163

spirit could evaluate people. He saw much with his eyes; he heard much with his ears, yet that was not important. He instead judged by the Wisdom of the Ages. The Spirit judged the wretched poor and the successful merchant without prejudice. A prostitute or a Pharisee, an intellectual or a mentally handicapped person, received the same consideration. He noted nothing of the outward man, only the inward heart. His judgment rose out of His own propriety and faithfulness. When He spoke, His Word always struck the mark; the wicked could not stand against Him. Jesus did not allow pretense nor did he wink at sin. He spoke to the root cause and still does because His motive is to set the hearer free.

If we are to be Life-givers, it is imperative that we judge by the Spirit of God not from our own prejudice. Life originates from the Lord. Even when our intention is good, we must realize our limitation.

> God told Moses, 'I'm in charge of mercy. I'm in charge of compassion.' Compassion doesn't originate in our bleeding hearts or moral sweat, but in God's mercy. (Rom.9) 2

Correction — A Positive Tool For Change

Positive correction is absolutely essential if we are to be like Jesus. Quite often it is necessary to correct others. How can we discern and bring correction without assaulting character or violating the person's dignity? This must be done with great care. The human tendency is to use correction and accusation to put others down in order to uplift oneself. Jesus was accused of deception, lawlessness, rebellion, blasphemy, and demon worship. His accusers were guilty of all of these including murder. It is essential to first deal with our own sinfulness in order to keep from presumption. Pride is removed when we realize the rebellion in another is ours also, or the pretense in our friend is a duplicate of our pretentiousness. Does this mean that no one should correct another? No! Just allow the Holy Spirit to show you your inner intentions, motives, and attitudes before you take the responsibility of correcting someone else.

Do not forget the great anguish associated with correction. Most of the time, hostility is the natural reaction. (Truth is often received negatively.) It is common to feel under attack, confused and defensive. The elaborate cover, so carefully constructed, is destroyed. Exposed, our mistakes, thoughtlessness, conniving, ungraciousness and weaknesses are laid open to outside scrutiny. A guilty verdict is hard to accept. Even if the truth is spoken with care, correction is very painful.

Most of us are acutely aware of our short comings. We have heard many accusations over our lifetime. We have found change difficult. Usually there is a need for encouragement (the bringing of strength and courage). All correction must be accompanied with tender mercy and loving kindness. Be careful. Be gentle. If you give your friend courage, she or he may open their hidden and secret places then you may have an opportunity to accurately minister truth and have it received with grace. This approach brings change.

How To Receive Correction
When corrected, we rarely have the poise to say, "You are right, show me my error, please forgive me, help me to change." Instead, we usually close down and wait for the offense to go away. It is hoped that a little "I'm sorry" will suffice and bring an end to the episode. However, appeasement does not lead to change. God's goal is to conform us to the image of the Son.

We must accept responsibility for our actions. If truly guilty we must admit the offense. Ask the Lord to reveal the attitudes and sinful patterns that led to the misbehavior. He will show you, *you*. He never just deals with the surface; He starts at the inner most part and uncovers the motivation that leads to the wrong and sinful behavior. Many do not change because they see and confess only the current misbehavior.

The offensive sinful root and the misbehavior resulting from it, must be acknowledged. It will not do to confess, "I've failed again." A general confession is nonspecific, and therefore, forgiveness is nonspecific. The offense must be stated. The resultant injury to others must be defined. Then you may humbly ask the Lord for forgiveness. In addition, you must go to the ones offended and repeat the procedure.

A caution: when asking for forgiveness, your spirit has to be humble and gracious. To demand forgiveness from others is presumptuous. I have heard, "You have to forgive me. Christ can't forgive you until you forgive me. What's with you anyway?" Forgiveness by the Lord or by anyone else is not a right, it is grace. Mercy is a gift.

Restitution must be made when appropriate. A girl involved in shoplifting asked, "How can I stop?" I said, "You need to return everything you have stolen, and then pay for the items." She replied, "Why would I ever do that? They would arrest me. Besides the stores carry insurance to cover their loss." Restitution was not her plan; she continued to steal. If restitution is made and the appropriate punishment received, the offense is usually not repeated.

The change in behavior must be authentic. Sometimes behavior changes just long enough to fool others, then the offense is repeated. This deepens the offense and indicates the root cause has not been addressed.

At the end of this process when repentance is genuine, you must forgive yourself because guilt can become a barrier to change. God forgives; usually people forgive, but we often do not forgive ourselves. God cannot release His mercy and forgiveness when we dish out punishment as if we were judge and jury. There is a time to examine behavior and then to repent. However, there also is a time to receive mercy and forgiveness. Don't be caught in this seeming righteous action. It is not righteous. It is an affront to God and to His forgiveness. Forgive yourself just as Christ has forgiven you.

This course of action is a real deterrent to repeated destructive conduct. It takes real courage to receive correction and carefully ask the Lord to bring change. This is the way out of guilt and shame into forgiveness and freedom.

The process of correction:
    Admission of guilt
    Confession to God and others
    Revelation of inner motives that caused the bad behavior
    Repentance for root causes and immediate offense.
    Request for forgiveness
    Acquisition of forgiveness

Restitution when appropriate
Acceptance of just punishment
Forgiveness of self.

Destructive Accusation

Accusations made from faultfinding, wound and kill the recipient.
The person is portrayed as bad, stupid, ugly and worthless. This
type of correction comes from critical negative insecure people
who try to maintain their own power. Faultfinding, name calling,
character assassination are the milieu. Abusive accusations leave
no room for change. "You are defective, bad to the core." Guilt
and shame are constantly present. These false accusations damage
self-esteem irreparably.

Please note: it is extremely important to discern the intent of the
criticism. In fault-finding the accuser exalts himself and destroys
the accused. The accuser feels he has a right and duty to undermine, criticize, and cast down the other. Positive correction is not
present when the one who 'knows' discredits and deposes the one
who is 'wrong.'

Never receive false and destructive criticism. It is given to injure.

How To Face Accusation
When accused seek the Lord.
Ask Him what you should do under the circumstances. Sometimes He will instruct you to leave the situation. At other times He
will help you clarify the relationship. He may tell you how to pray
and why. Be responsive to His direction and wisdom.

Know what is true.
Are you Bad? Hopeless? Ugly? Worthless? Know what the Word of
God says about you. Know your worth, your limitations. Do not
accept injurious, cutting words of condemnation. Listen to the
Father; what is He saying?

Discern the intent of the accuser.
Is the intent to injure, wound or discard you so that someone
might be 'lord?' Are you made to feel crazy, wrong, inept? Does
the accuser resist counsel? If the intent of the accuser is to hurt,
do not cower. Seek the Lord for guidance.

Do not compromise to appease a harmful accuser.
First of all, it never brings resolution. Second, you will lose your
bearings and be disoriented. Third, you will be injured. Fourth,
the accuser has learned that it pays to intimidate.

How To Overcome Satan, The Accuser Of The Brethren
In addition to human criticism, Satan accuses us. (Rev.10:12) His
voice sounds like this: *"You are stupid. You call yourself a Christian, some witness. Thought Jesus made a difference? Listen to
yourself. Same old person, you never change. You can't quit
even the littlest bad habit. God gets tired of you. Look at that,
failed again. Ask for forgiveness, again! When will it ever end?
You need to be punished. You didn't do your best. God doesn't
love you. How could He? He didn't heal you either because you
don't deserve it."* Our own voice of doubt and fear join this cho-
rus of condemnation. This accusation can go on night and day,
night and day for an entire lifetime unless the weapons provided
for us by God are used to defeat the Accuser.

The accuser of the brethren is "overcome by the blood of the
Lamb, by the word of our testimony, and giving up our lives even
in death." (Rev. 10:12)

The blood of the Lamb cleanses us from guilt and shame.

"If we walk in the light as He is in the light, we have fellowship
with one another, and the blood of Jesus Christ His Son cleanses
us from all sin." (1Jn.1:7) How does this apply? Bring all sin to
the Lord and work to restore all relationships that have been dam-
aged. How we get along with others is a good gauge of how well
we are doing. There is something wrong if others are constantly
offended and mad at us. Ask the Lord to reveal what is amiss,
acknowledge it, and repent. "If we confess our sins, He is faithful
and just to forgive our sins and to cleanse us from all unrighteousness." (IJn.1:9) The crime is canceled. You might say, "Wait a
minute, I still feel guilty." Feeling guilty is not the same as being
guilty. Our real sin is forgiven. Satan, the accuser, intimidates and
oppresses with accusations about offenses that have already been
forgiven. Give him no room; admit when you are wrong and do
something about it. Then discard the accusatory voices that whisper discouragement.

The accuser is defeated when we testify to the amazing transforming presence of God in our lives.

Testimony is the evidence given, a witness given of something experienced. We are the testimony to His presence upon the earth. It is not so much what we say, it is our life. The New Testament contains the testimony of the early believers; we are the testimony now!

Death is a weapon also. When accused it is natural to hold fast to everything precious. "No one can take my reputation, my job, my position, my possessions. I won't let them!" We will be afraid of both life and death if we still cling to the Things of Man. Our happiness then will depend upon possessions, control of people, and the management of our circumstances for our advantage. This is not God's way.

We become invincible when we relinquish everything to the Lord.

The accuser of the brethren, the god of this world, loses his hold when we belong to the King. Our life is an outflow of our love for the Lord. Circumstances do not matter. Our ordinary lives are the stage to show forth His Life and defeat the accuser of the brethren.

"For to me, to live is Christ, and to die is gain. (Phil.1:21)

NOTES:

Section 4
Follow Him Into Life

Chapter 10
The Wilderness and the Test
* Silence, Solitude, Simplicity: There are several books I would rec-ommend for additional information about solitude, silence and simplicity.
James Buckingham, *A Way Through the Wilderness,* (Grand Rapids, Mich. Zondervan Corp. 1983)
Richard Foster, *Celebration of Discipline*, (San Francisco:Harper and Row 1978) p.84-95.
Gordon MacDonald, *Restoring Joy To Your Inner World*, (New York, Inspirational Press, 1998)
p. 302-312.
Henri Nouwen, *The Three Movements of Spiritual Life, Reaching Out*, (New York, Doubleday and Co. 1975) Movement from loneli-ness to solitude.
Eugene Peterson, *Working the Angles, (Grand Rapids, Mich., Eerd-mans Publ. Co., 1993) p.63-83.*

Chapter 11
Arena of Conflict
1 Peterson, *The Message* p.33.
"He who is not with Me is against Me, and he who does not gather with me scatters abroad. (Mt.12:30)
2 Peterson, *The Message p.32.*
"As they went out, behold, they brought to Him a man, mute and demon-possessed. And when the demon was cast out, the mute spoke. And the multitudes marveled, saying, "It was never seen like this in Israel!" But the Pharisees said, "He casts out demons by the ruler of the demons." (Mt. 11:32-34 NKJ)
3 Peterson, *The Message,* p. 32.
"And behold, there was a man who had a withered hand. And they asked Him, saying, "Is it lawful to heal on the Sabbath?" — that they might accuse Him. Then He said to them, "What man is there among you who has one sheep, and if it falls into a pit on the Sabbath, will not lay hold of it and lift it out? Of how much more value then is a man than a sheep? Therefore it is lawful to do good on the Sabbath." Then He said to the man, "Stretch out

170

your hand." And he stretched it out, and it was restored as whole as the others. Then the Pharisees went out and plotted against Him, how they might destroy Him. (Mt.12:10-14 NKJ)

Chapter 13
Betrayal
1 Sandford, John and Paula, *Healing the Wounded Spirit*, (New Jersey, Bridge Publ. Co.) pg. 254-255.

Chapter 14
Captivity and Freedom
1 *Webster's New World Dictionary,* p.895
2 Peterson, *The Message*, p. 154
"And behold, there was a woman who had a spirit of infirmity eighteen years, and was bent over and could in no way raise herself up. But when Jesus saw her, He called her to Him and said to her, "woman, you are loosed from your infirmity." And He laid His hands on her, and immediately she was made straight, and glorified God." (Lk.13:11-13)
3 Strongs, #8074 p.118 Hebrew/Chaldee Dictionary
4 Peterson, *The Message, p.373-374.*
"But we have this treasure in earthen vessels, that the excellence of the power may be of God and not of us. We are hard-pressed on every side, yet not crushed; we are perplexed, but not in despair; persecuted, but not forsaken; struck down, but not destroyed always carrying about in the body the dying of the Lord Jesus, that the life of Jesus also may be manifested in our body. (IICor.4:7-11 NKJ)

Chapter 15
Accusation
1 Peterson, *The Message p.321.*
"Therefore He has mercy on whom He wills, and whom He wills He hardens. (Rom.9:18 NKJ)
2 Peterson, *The Message,* p. 229.
" Pilate therefore said to Him, "Are You a king then?" Jesus answered, "You say rightly that I am a king. For this cause I was born, and for this cause I have come into the world, that I should bear witness to the truth. Everyone who is of the truth hears My voice." (Jn.18:37 NKJ)

THE
CENTERPIECE

"When His soul has been made an offering for sin,
then he shall have a multitude of children,
many heirs...
" (Is. 53:10)

chapter

16

THE

VICTOR

"God laid on him the guilt and sins of every one of us!"
(Is. 53:6)

"He was brought as a lamb to the slaughter..." (Is.53:7)

On this sixth day of the week, time split into two parts, before and after the death of Jesus. He alone can occupy this fulcrum of time. Jesus, filled with Life, is sacrificed by the death-givers.

The event on Golgotha is nothing like the sterile renditions portrayed in books or on film. Here all the wicked, evil forces of hell gathered in one place. Vicious, vile, hateful men cursed, mocked, and tortured Jesus. Leave the television programs, the soft chairs, the nice clean environment and enter the place of the skull, Golgotha. Leave the twentieth century, come with me to the cross, the fulcrum of all time. It is here we come to know the difference between a death-giver and the Life-giver. Here we witness the Love of God at war with the Evil of this world. Watch the the battle between Life and death.

* * *

The most innocent, wonder-filled, powerful man to live, hung on the cross, naked, bleeding, and dying. Jesus, the perfect image of the Father, pinned to a tree, heard the blasphemy of the death-givers.

174

If you are the Christ...
If you are the chosen of God...the King of Israel...
If you are the Son of God...

Save Yourself!
Come down from the cross!
That we may see and believe.

The religious leaders said,

> He saved others; Himself He cannot save.
> He trusted in God; let Him deliver Him now if He will
> have Him; for He said, 'I am the Son of God.'(Mt.27:39-41)

Come down from the cross!

Jesus gave them no sign. It was too late!

Even before the crucifixion on Golgotha, Jesus had been scourged, leaving His back ripped open, raw and bleeding. Beating and spitting on Him, the soldiers made sport of Him. (Mt.27:28-31) They dressed Him as a king and then knelt before him in pretended worship. They were powerful and mighty, or so they thought. Following orders of an earthly governor, they nailed Jesus to the cross. The Mighty King let them do it.

The iniquitous crowd gathered. The human race, stripped of its nicety, showed forth immense evil. People passed the execution scene yelling vile words of derision and mockery. The dying thief ridiculed Jesus and died. The calloused soldiers, detached from the horror of the "Skull Place," rolled the dice. The religious, dressed in the garb of priest and scribe, were glad for this day. Thinking him a fool, they were fools. Thinking him powerless, they were tools of Satan. Thinking Him presumptuous and an impostor, they presumed to know God. All the horror of this place can be described in one word, SIN. It is not an idea nor is it just a little worldliness. This was human hatred and rebellion unleashed upon God. This is Golgotha, not a nice, gentle scene. It is violent; it is evil.

The cross exposed evil.
The cross is the vivid picture of God's love and man's evil.
The Cross is the Centerpiece of the Things of God.

Here the Life-giver, the perfect, holy, glorious Lamb gave His Life as a sacrifice.

* * *

The human race is much the same from century to century. We are represented by those at the scene. Can you identify yourself in the crowd? Are you one of those who cried, "Blessed is He Who Comes in the Name of the Lord, Hosanna in the Highest?" Then, the very next day, yelled, "Crucify Him, Crucify Him" at His trial? Surely you are not one of the false witnesses, paid to lie, or one of the executioners? Perhaps you are one who just watched the spectacle, a bit curious. Are you more like the one who cried, "Oh, no! Not Jesus! He must not die. He healed me!" You might be one of the religious, or maybe a detached soldier, or like cursing Peter. Are you one who sat below the cross and gambled for a token souvenir? Maybe you are like Mary, the mother of Jesus, who mourned the loss of her son.

This place undresses death from its mortuary camouflage. Be horrified by Jesus' agony. Watch the battle between life and death, good and evil, freedom and captivity. Take a look at this scene, smell the stench of death, see the agony, listen to the laughter. Ask yourself, "What would I do?" Would I turn away, unable to endure the gory, ugly mess? Would I weep? Curse? Gamble? Laugh? Ridicule? Would I think: "I am not like any who are here"? We are present at this place of death. Do not leave. Do not hide your face. Look at the Life-giver and remember the evil of the death-givers. Can you see the difference between those around the cross and the one on the cross?

He commanded us to follow Him as Life-givers, however, we cannot endure this place. He alone gives His Life. Even if I stepped forward and begged, "Jesus, don't die, not for me. I deserve to die. You are too precious to die in my place." He would say, "I alone can give my life for you. Your own evil prevents you from being a perfect sacrifice. My Father would not accept your offering. Your life would not prevent your eternal death. I alone am the Life-giver; you belong to me and as I die, your sin, your wickedness, your rebellion, your lust, will be put to death. I am perfect and my sacrifice will satisfy the Father. If you belong to me, all is forgiven."

Death flowed toward Jesus. Grief and sorrow, transgressions and diseases, the iniquity and rebellion of us all, was laid upon Jesus. (Is.53:4-6) The Lamb took our sin.

While He died, Jesus, the Life-giver, poured Love upon us. He looked at the mob and pitied those who hated Him. He wept, "Oh, my beloved!" "Oh Father, forgive them for they do not know what they are doing!" (Lk.23:34) "Forgive the religious, the curious, the gambling soldiers, the mocking, jeering crowd, the weeping women, the denying Peter, the fearful. Forgive all who do not love." This prayer, a call for mercy from the Father, released us from condemnation.

The Life-giver loves. He is Forgiveness.

Jesus knew that His mother suffered. Mary remembered the words spoken to her long ago by Simeon, "Behold, this Child is destined for the fall and rising of many in Israel, and for a sign which will be spoken against (yes, a sword will pierce through your own soul also), that the thoughts of many hearts may be revealed." (Lk.2:34-35) She watched her son's agony. The anguish in her soul was unbearable. Mary wept. Jesus looked down at her. "John, care for Mary and be her son." (Jn.19:25-27)

The Life-giver loves. He is Loving-kindness.

He was crucified between two thieves. One cursed and blasphemed; the other called out for mercy, "Lord, remember me when you come into your kingdom!" Jesus promised to save him.

The Life-giver loves. He is Salvation.

The outer world disappeared. Jesus drew into the inner world which had been filled with the Father. *The Father was not there!* His spirit was empty. He called to the Father, *"My God, My God, why have you forsaken me!"*(Mk.15:34) His Father, the source of Life, no longer sustained Him. He cried, *"It is finished!"*(Jn.19:30)

He whispered, *"Father into your hand I commit my Spirit."*(Lk.23:46)

The Father heard the Son.

The Life-giver loves. He is the Lamb slain before the foundation of the earth. (Rev.13:8)

The Father's power descended to Golgotha. Darkness deepened; the ground convulsed and broke apart; rocks split in two; the earth roared and groaned; the sun withdrew. In the temple, the Holy of Holies stood exposed, the great tapestry torn from top to bottom. (Lk.23:45) With the death of the Lamb, God ended the old way of entrance into His Presence; a new way began.

The Life-giver is Love. He is the Revelation of the Father.

Power to bring life out of death entered the graves of those already dead. They came alive and were seen in the city.

The Life-giver loves. He is Resurrection.

Power to believe entered the spectators. The gentile soldier declared, "Truly this Man was the Son of God!" (Mk.15:39) The crowd beat their breasts!

The Life-giver loves. He is the Victor.

In death, Jesus exhibited all the lessons of Life. He left all: his friends, his mother, his beloved disciples, and Peter. He was stripped of all comfort, all modesty, all riches, all power.

All the Things of Man were left behind at the cross.

The years of preparation laid a foundation of truth. The Word flowed through His Spirit in his agony. (Jn.1:14)

The Word was fulfilled at the cross.

The devil waited for an opportunity to finish his temptation. The Lamb of God, hanging on a tree in the middle of all the hordes of Satan, heard the taunt, *"If you are the Christ..." "If you are the cho-*

sen of God...""If you are the King of the Jews...""If you are the Son of God..."

The ultimate test was given at the cross.

The Lamb of God fought the forces of hell, unbelief, the kingdom of man, resistance to truth. God was at war.

The Arena of Conflict raged at the cross.

Here on the cross Jesus absorbed all evil and returned love, care, and salvation. He poured out the Father's love. His betrayal, capture, and accusation did not turn Him to bitterness and hatred. He remained free to pray, to forgive, to care, to save, and to reveal the Father. He exhibited the lessons of Captivity and Freedom.

The Model of Love is shown at the Cross.

How then do we follow Jesus? We begin at His death. We remain detached from the love of God when we do not comprehend His sacrifice. Here God is at war with evil. He is Victor over Sin which leads to death. Do we see His sacrifice as the ultimate expression of love?

Transformation begins when we see and experience His incredible love. Power is released deep within us. At a depth unseen, our inner core groans and breaks apart. We then see, and cry out, *"Oh God, what love!"* Like the tapestry which separated the Holy of Holies from entry, our inner hard, impenetrable places split apart. We are delivered from death and find open access to God. Death within us vanishes, and Life springs forth. We are in Him, and He is in us.

God draws us into His Presence at the Cross.

The Victor Gives Us Life
As we respond to the Love of God, He opens to us more and more of His Life. This is not a simple one-time event. It happens throughout our whole lifetime as we come to know Him. He takes our life and invades it with His Love. He opens to us the Things of God; the Things of Man no longer entice us. We die to our old ways. We learn to embrace our limitations and strengths as

we carry them through life. He forms His image in us as we desire to be like Him. The Word guides us into Truth. Conversation with Him is a natural outflow of His Presence. When the test comes, we remember and know that God alone is able to keep us. In the arena of conflict we see the power of God prevail. We open our inner spirit and allow Him to love others through us. It is our delight to listen to the inner voice of the Father speaking to us of His hidden secrets. When falsely betrayed and accused, we remain free from bitterness, able to forgive, to love, to grieve. We weep for and love those with whom we live, who are sometimes our enemy. He gives us the things we need, security, recognition, love, and adventure. He gives Life, so abundantly it surprises us. We are eternally thankful.

> "We are His workmanship, created in Christ Jesus for good works, which God prepared beforehand that we should walk in them." (Eph.2:10)

Jesus alone is the mighty Lamb of God dwelling at the right hand of the Father, who is worshipped and adored in heaven and on the earth. With His sacrifice, the cross, the symbol of death, is God's Love given so that we might live.

* * *

Joseph of Arimathea and Nicodemus, the Pharisee, took Jesus, the Lamb, the seed of Life, from the cross and placed Him into the ground. With the work of salvation complete, God the Father waited...

The Lamb was dead — buried in the earth.

Sabbath began — It was evening, the beginning of the seventh day.

Those who loved Him cried — and cried — and cried.

> "...unless a grain of wheat falls into the ground and dies, it remains alone..." (Jn.12:24)

S A B B A T H

"Then they took the body of Jesus, and bound it in strips of linen with the spices, as the custom of the Jews is to bury. Now in the place where He was crucified there was a garden, and in the garden a new tomb in which no one had yet been laid. So there they laid Jesus, because of the Jews' Preparation Day, for the tomb was nearby. (Jn.19:39-42)

God instituted the Sabbath at the very beginning of time. (Sabbath means *cessation*.) On each of six days God created; on the seventh, He rested and was refreshed. (Ex.31:17) This rhythm, this pattern of six days of work, a day of rest, six days of work, a day of rest has continued since that time. Not filled with work, this space...of time...was for rest. During this rest mankind was to worship God.

Jesus had finished His work of salvation. The Sabbath of God began. We are invited into this rest. However, rest, (doing nothing) is not comfortable. Struggle and toil, worry and strife seem more natural, however, they are not of God. Agitation and inability to rest often point to unbelief. God urges us to follow his rhythm and rest, assured that He is in control.

In between death and resurrection is a space, a slack time. One chapter of life ends, and another has not yet begun. Although this pause specifically applies to the death and resurrection of Jesus, we also experience this empty space when something extremely important ends, and nothing takes its place. It is in this pause that much is revealed. The temporal decays; the eternal remains. The Things of Man disintegrate; the Things of God continue. During this time it is impossible to even imagine the plan of God. We are forced by circumstances to quit everything and wait to see the next chapter. This pause is Sabbath. *

* * *

The Lamb buried in the dark tomb, like a seed in the ground, waited for the Father's call. It was Sabbath, in heaven, in Israel, and in the tomb. Jesus had finished His assignment as Life-giver. The Father had revealed and given His Son to the World. God had accomplished this part of His agenda. Other events would soon occur, but here was an empty space where God the Son was still. God the Father confidently waited. "A multitude of children, many heirs..." (Is. 53:10) would soon be the dwelling place of God's Spirit. All was in readiness. God's plan would be completed. Nothing was amiss. Out of the grave would spring Life.

The Strife of Man
Those who loved Him had no peace at all for their Messiah was dead. Peter was in tremendous pain, unable to bring recent events to any reasonable resolution. Everything he thought true, proved to be in error.

The exciting life with his extraordinary friend was over. The terror of the scene of the bleeding dying savior played in his mind again and again; Jesus was dead. *"The loss, the loss"* Peter went into the night and wept. *"Oh God, oh, God...I don't understand! Oh God, How can I live? It couldn't have happened...just watching Him struggle for each breath, and then to see Him give His love even as He died. No, Oh, No. He was dead. Dead. His love had been strong and consuming like fire, yet filled with comfort and deep penetrating honesty. I was so sure I would never leave Him. I'm worse than Judas. Oh God..."* Peter lay on the cold earth. *"God why? Why did you let it happen?"* The anguish of the crushing pain trapped him in deep black despair. Jesus told of this place as He rebuked the Pharisees who asked Him for a sign. He said,

> An evil and adulterous generation seeks after a sign, and no sign will be given to it except the sign of the prophet Jonah. For as Jonah was three days and three nights in

182

the belly of the great fish, so will the Son of Man be three days and three nights in the heart of the earth.
   (Mt. 12:39-40)

Peter, so to speak, was in the belly of the fish, buried like Jesus. *"If only he was dead like Judas. What was he to do ?...Ohhhhh...God..."* Confused regretful thoughts flooded in, *"If only...if I could have...now it is too late."* There was no relief; nothing made sense.

After the night of horror, morning began. Like Peter, the followers of Jesus were overwhelmed. Oppressed by the spirit of death, they wept or sat silent waiting for the end of the Sabbath so that they could go to the tomb. It was a long, long day, buried alive in the belly of the fish. They were too confused and despairing to even remember:
   the faithfulness of a Living God.
   the promise of Messiah, "I will rise again!"
   the mighty God in control of even this.

Before this time of extreme pain and turmoil, Jesus had prayed. "Oh Father, keep them from the evil one (Jn.17:15) and do not let their faith fail. (Lk.22:31) I want them to be with Us, to come to where I am going. Soon they will be one with Us." (Jn.17:9 author's paraphrase)

God the Father protected them during Sabbath.

* * *

Why the Space Between Death and Resurrection?
God demands a Sabbath, a cessation from struggle and strife so that it is clear that He does the work. It is quite natural for Christians to strive to be good people and do the right thing. Often however, this can lead to a continual expenditure of effort to achieve greater and greater perfection. Once the spiritual foundation has been established, it is on to holiness, witnessing, fasting and prayer. It is believed that God requires all of this, and only then, does He acknowledge and approve of the believer. This is not true. None of this work forces God to approve of us. God already loves His children no matter the perfection.

God has a rest for the people of God. Spiritual life is not strife, work, and struggle. He alone can do the work of the ministry. He is the one who gives Life. He alone can save. He alone can heal. He alone can forgive sin. All that we do must come from the outflow of His Life within us. We must make the transition from natural effort to resurrection Life. He has finished the work of salvation. The work days are over. Sabbath has begun. Our work is to enter into His Rest. This is Sabbath.

This rest and confidence in the Lord does not come easily. God sets about to show us our limitations and inability to control anything. We often experience this awful lesson in the midst of major transition. Although not equivalent to the enormous loss of Jesus, our despair seems similar in the midst of personal catastrophe. This is not like the wilderness and the test where God steps back and places us in a stark environment, to test our foundation. This is not the desolate place where God draws us to Himself. Here, the Father waits; He seems to do nothing. God uses this painful time to strip us. Satan may want to sift us as wheat. Be assured, the Lord knows our dire need.

Buried alive in circumstances beyond our contol, in the belly of the fish, nothing makes sense; loss is overwhelming. Because of our limited comprehension, it is impossible to see God at work. What appeared true in the past, no longer applies. Prayer seems useless; obedience to the voice of God, brings no joy. Faith erodes away. We may even have thoughts of leaving the Lord. We try to pray, read the word, work hard, mind our own business. Still confusion and grief over-ride everything. Memories may bring excruciating pain. There are no happy days filled with laughter, fun, sunshine. Answered prayer and tender miraculous touches from His Majesty are just memories of another time. Now, in painful contrast, life is aberrant. Spiritual strength fades. Hope dies. Darkness descends.

It is difficult to see what makes us secure until it is removed. We often do not realize our vulnerability and limitation. God shows us our weakness, our inability to effect change.

The lesson of Sabbath — In the tomb, we can do nothing to change the circumstances.

We are helpless. However, God is in control and keeps us from the spirit of death that ever hovers near to crush the will to live. We are buried alive and wish we were dead. Peter's despair and

Jonah's experience in the belly of the fish, are ours:

> Out of the belly of Sheol I cried, and You heard my voice.
> For You cast me into the deep, into the heart of the seas,
> and the floods surrounded me; all Your billows and Your
> waves passed over me. Then I said, *'I have been cast out
> of Your sight; yet I will look again toward your holy tem-
> ple.'* The waters surrounded me, even to my soul; the deep
> closed around me; weeds were wrapped around my head.
> I went down to the moorings of the mountains; the earth
> with its bars closed behind me forever; yet You have
> brought up my life from the pit, O Lord, my God.
>   (Jonah 2:2-9)

The lesson of Sabbath — God is in control of everything.

In our complete helplessness, there is nothing, absolutely nothing, we can do to rescue ourselves. God brings an end to all of
our schemes. The good spiritual man comes to know that it is not
his effort to be good that saves him. The Godly woman realizes
that her performance of kind acts and generous hospitality do not
keep her. God allows the loss to reveal our utter inability to
comprehend the Things of God.

In the tomb the Things of Man disintegrate. The Spirit of God
invades the emptiness. In the darkness of despair, the eternal
things gain advantage over all others. Jonah turned to the Lord in
his desperate hour, however, he remained in the whale until God
delivered him. (Jon.2:10)   God alone can deliver.

Until we see our weakness and limitations as a human, we are
unable to move beyond death to resurrection. The next phase in
the Agenda of God requires us to enter Kingdom territory. Everything that comes out of the grave is eternal and originates from
that realm. It is impossible for us to be at one with God as long as
we think we are in control. We experience the Sabbath, the rest of
God, when we know that there is nothing we can do to change
the plan of God. We quit, give up. Our plan ends, and we are
forced to wait for revelation.

The pause between the disaster and the answer seems an eternity.
Jonah in the belly of the fish could not escape, and Peter in
despair had no hope of redemption. They could do nothing.

The lesson of Sabbath — We must wait.

The pain continues. The old schemes do not bring relief. The flesh screams. He allows all of this to bring a transition from human strength to His Life. The pain during the pause brings an end to human plans. No man can endure the tomb, the belly of the fish, and survive unless God breaths life back into him. No one can sustain belief unless the Father gives it to him. No follower of Jesus knows God's faithfulness until he is delivered from the fish, the tomb. It is here we are separated unto His purposes. God alone preserves life in a seed that is buried in the ground. God alone brings Life to us in this desperate place. This is Sabbath, the pause between death and resurrection.

Remember grace precedes us. Jesus said, "Simon, Satan has asked for you, that he may sift you as wheat. But I have prayed for each of you, that your faith should not fail; and when you have returned to Me, strengthen your brethren." (Lk.22:31)

The Lesson of Sabbath — Jesus has prayed for us that our faith will not fail.

Jesus' life and death were irrefutable evidence that He was Messiah. This left no room for man's plan. The wait between the incomprehensible event of the death of the Son of God, and his resurrection took away man's pride in his ability to figure things out. This prepared the way for the Things of God, Life out of death. Resurrection is beyond our scheme of things, the Things of Man.

The lesson of Sabbath — God is at work even in the pause —
There remains therefore a rest for the people of God. For he who has entered His rest has himself also ceased from his works as God did from His.
(Heb.4:9-10)

Remember the faithfulness of God in all circumstances —
wait — do not lose hope —
wait — expectantly —
wait for the greatest day of all!

RESURRECTION

A great earthquake rolled across the city as Creative Power, awesome, unlimited, unfathomable Power, from the spiritual realm, touched the Earth at the garden tomb. Angels descended to the sepulcher. Pilate's guards were as dead men.

The Voice of the Father entered the body of the Son. Jesus, filled with Life, came out of the tomb omnipotent and triumphant over His enemies. He, the mighty Lamb of God, had ransomed and redeemed all from the power of the grave. (Hosea 13:14)

The heavenly realm was filled with great shouts and music, worship and glorious praise. "The Son, the Lamb, is worthy, is worthy, is worthy!"

The Father glorified the Son.

* * *

Beloved of the Lord, we know the story. Let us not become so familiar with the facts that we brush aside its significance. Jesus was invaded with resurrection Power, Life from the spiritual realm, Eternal Life. No longer confined to an earthly body Jesus was able to be on earth, in heaven, everywhere, all at one time. As a result, He is always present and therefore, we can personally know Him.

Jesus comes with this abounding Life into our "belly of the fish." He can invade the hard places in our hearts. He can come into the mind and enlighten our thoughts. He can repair the damage done by the enemy. Stop and realize the miracle and rejoice. Jesus comes out of the grave and reveals Himself to us so that we might know God. This power changes us from those who live by our own strength to those who live by the Spirit.

* * *

Vignettes Of Resurrection
We can see little glimpses of the resurrected Jesus as He met the disciples. He did simple things; He spoke simple words. Miraculously as He spoke and fellowshipped with His friends, Eternal Life overcame death. What had no life came alive. Where there was no faith, belief occurred. What was natural became spiritual. Watch and see resurrection power as it transformed the followers of Jesus. Catch a glimpse of the moment when Jesus appeared. In that instant despair and unbelief vanished.

The First Lord's Day —
The disciples were still in the belly of the fish. There was no relief from the crushing sorrow. They had forgotten the promise, "I will rise from the dead." (Lk.24:7)

The Women
The lamenting, grief-stricken Mary, Mary Magdeline, and Salome carried embalming spices to the tomb. (Lk.24:10) Duty was the only thing left: to tend to the dead, to make the rotting flesh smell better, to look one last time at this man. They approached the tomb and found the great stone removed. He was gone. The angels declared, "He is risen! He is not here! Do not be afraid!" Terrified, the women fled this place where the glorious realm touched the earth.

188

We, like the women, turn to remember dead dreams, fanciful schemes, and idealized philosophies when in the desperate hopeless place. We then try to recapture their "magic." We cry and lament. Duty and tradition are of no use.

Would you have been afraid at the empty tomb? I think so. When God does the impossible we are usually terrified and run from the miraculous presence of God. Fortunately, the Father is not surprised. He says, "Do not be afraid." "I will come to you again." Fear is the response to resurrection power.

Mary
Mary lingered. A man asked, "Why are you weeping, Mary?"(Jn.20:15-16) When she heard her name, she knew that it was Jesus who spoke to her. Unbelief and despair vanished. She fell at His feet and held on tightly. He said, "Do not cling to me. I have not yet ascended to My Father. Go, say to the brethren, I am ascending to My Father and your Father, and to My God and your God!" (Jn.20:17)

We, like Mary, *know* the Lord when the resurrected Christ addresses us by name. God is not an abstraction. He identifies Himself as, "I am the Lord, *your* God." Jesus says the Father is *our* Father, and we are *His* children. He calls — Listen for your name. Reassuringly He might say, "Do not be afraid. Come here, my child. I love to be with you."

It is His personal care and attention, His love, that draws us to Himself, to Life.

The disciples did not believe the women's story (Lk.24:11) for they were still in darkness, the belly of the whale. However, Peter and John ran to the tomb and found it empty. (Lk.24:12) Their conversations were filled with questions, questions and more questions. The disciples' sorrow had turned to confusion because spiritual things are spiritually discerned.

Emmaus
Two of the believers left for their home in Emmaus. As they walked away from Jerusalem they were joined by another traveler. He asked, "What are you discussing?" They answered,

Don't you know what happened in the city this week? Are you the only one who hasn't heard how He, the acclaimed Messiah, was put to death on a cross, but now some have seen Him, and others say that his body is missing. We were hoping that it was He who was going to redeem Israel. Now we are still captives of the Romans and our hope of redemption is gone! (Lk.24:13-35)

The traveler rebuked them, "O foolish men, slow of heart to believe..." He then expounded the scripture of the Old Testament which spoke of this day, this time, this Messiah. His words set their hearts aflame. "Please come to dinner and tell us more!" While dining with them, He took, blessed, and broke the bread and gave it to them. Their eyes opened, and they *knew* Jesus. Unbelief vanished. They were delivered from the grave.

Jesus travels along with us even if we do not *see* Him. He chides us for unbelief and then opens the meaning of scripture. Jesus takes common elements (like the bread) to reveal His presence. When we *see* Him, confusion and unbelief disappear. We are changed.

Deep within us, the Word spoken to us by the Lord works to change unbelief to faith.

The Disciples
The disciples gathered in Galilee. Some grieved; some rejoiced; some doubted.
They waited —
He said He would come — And then —
He was with them.
They were terrified!

"Peace to you! You are unbelieving and hard of heart for not believing the witnesses. Why are you troubled? Why do doubts arise in your hearts? Behold my hands and feet. Handle me and see. It is I myself. No ghost has flesh and bones. May I join you for dinner? Remember I told you that all that was foretold of the Messiah in the Old Writings would be fulfilled? "(Lk.24:38)

He then opened their understanding of the scriptures. He was alive. Oh, how they marveled at what they had witnessed and heard. Their despair turned to joy.

Thomas, not present when Jesus appeared, was still unbelieving. Several days later Jesus returned and called to Thomas, "Touch me, put your fingers into the wounds in my hands." Thomas *believed*, "My Lord and My God!"

Do not miss the implication. Jesus made belief possible. The disciples touched Him; they ate with Him; He opened their understanding of scriptures. When you are unbelieving, when you think Jesus is not there, or that God does not care, or that He could not understand your doubts and confusion, each time remember, He makes belief possible. Ask Him to reveal Himself to you. Ask Him to open the Word to you. Ask Him to come.

Jesus makes belief possible!

Peter
 Peter missed the point of the resurrection and decided to return to fishing. He could not see how the resurrected Jesus affected his life. He could not see his extraordinary future. "Come on Nathaniel and Thomas let's go fishing!" (Jn.21:2)   As they came close to the shore, someone yelled, "How's the fishing?" They answered, "We fished all night; no fish at all." The inquirer shouted, "Throw the net on the other side of the boat!" John shouted, "It's the Lord!" They caught a multitude of fish. (Jn.21:4-7) Peter jumped into the sea and swam to shore yelling, "It's the Lord! It's the Lord!" Jesus had cooked breakfast for them. The Lord of Glory, the Great and Mighty King enjoyed breakfast on the sea shore with his friends.

Peter had no peace for he needed to be forgiven and healed. He remembered vividly the words that Jesus had spoken to him. "You will deny me." (Lk.22:34)   He had been so sure of his loyalty. Jesus did not let him stay miserable.

> "Simon, son of Jonah, do you love Me more than these?"
> "Yes Lord, you know that I love you."
> " Feed My lambs."
> "Simon, son of Jonah, do you love Me?"
> "Yes Lord, you know that I love you."
> "Feed My sheep."

"Simon, son of Jonah, do you love Me?:
"Lord, you know all things, you know I love you."
"Feed my sheep. When you were younger, you girded
yourself and walked where you wished; but when you are
old, you will stretch out your hands, and another will gird
you and carry you where you do not wish."
"Follow me!" (Jn.21:15-19)

Peter then knew he was forgiven. The regret, the agony, the pain
of his failure left. The Lord had not given up on him. Jesus had
asked him to openly declare his love, and he had done it. Peter
was freed from his failure. Jesus rejoiced. Peter rejoiced; he
would now follow the Lord, even in death.

Jesus is with us in times of failure. If we try to return to ordinary
life (fishing), we will find it impossible. Jesus does not let go, give
up, or allow us to hide. He sometimes gets our attention with "a
multitude of fish." He gives us opportunity to once again confess
our love. Fellowship with the servant King reminds us of his graciousness. He does not allow a permanent break in relationship
with Him.

*His resurrected Life invades the deepest places of regret, failure,
sin, and heals the wound.*

* * *

The Gift Of God The Holy Spirit
The believers needed the Holy Spirit in order to begin the next
phase of the Agenda of God. Even though they believed, they
could not *see* spiritually. They still were unable to do anything
spiritual, anything filled with His power, anything that produced
Life. The Holy Spirit was the completion of the circuit.

Jesus commanded, "Go to Jerusalem and wait for the Holy Spirit!
Welcome Him, for He is the promise of the Father."
(Lk.24:46-49, Jn.20:22)

They waited —
the Spirit came —
He was in the room.
He was upon them.

He was around them.
He was in them.
He was spilling out of them.

They were baptized in the Mighty Spirit. He did not go away.
They remained and lived in the element (the Holy Spirit.)

They were filled with God Himself.

* * *

The Holy Spirit equips us for Life. Without Him nothing spiritual
is possible. He *empowers* our words of testimony so that others
can hear our witness and receive Life. (Lk.24:48-49)

He constantly *comforts* us every day, every moment for we often
are discouraged, afraid, wounded, and lost. His Comfort is wonderful. He calls us by name. He reassures us that God loves us.
(Jn.14:16-18)

It is God's Spirit that *keeps* us from the enemy. He shows us what
is true, and what is false; what is evil, and what is good; what is
wise, and what is foolish. (Jn.14:25-31) Do you realize what a marvelous gift He is?

He *teaches* about the Father and the Son. (Jn.14:26) He translates
the Word into Life for us. Without Him the Word would remain
just stories, events in the past. He helps us to remember all that
God has done, historically and personally.

He *seeks* for the unbelievers to bring them life. (Jn.16:8)

Most of all He *loves* the Son. He is the one who helps us worship,
who inspires praise, who releases the church to magnify the Lord.
(Jn.16:14)

Do not skip over this. The death and resurrection of Jesus make
belief possible. The Spirit enables us to live as Jesus commanded.
I encourage you to know Jesus as the mighty One who baptizes in
the Holy Spirit. If you do not know the Spirit, ask for Him to
come; you will not be denied.

The Christian life must be lived in complete dependence upon the Spirit. He is the One who lives inside us. He is the One who does the work. He is the One who loves. He is the One who has all wisdom and gives some of it to us. Without Him we do not know how to live and what to do, nor do we have Life to give to others. He is the Life of God, the Source of Life.

Resurrection life is not a series of steps leading to super human men or women. This Life is a continuum of learning. It is like entering, always entering, into a dimension which is deeper, higher, larger, greater, always expanding. To know God is beyond our finite understanding, and yet, we can *know* Jesus. It is the Holy Spirit who continually opens new hidden places to us. Gradually, a new and better way of life emerges. Each step is supernatural. Each part of our plan comes into death, stays there, and is transformed by resurrection. We leave behind the things of man and, bit by bit, understand and participate in the Things of God.

Jesus, the Seed of Life, gave His Life so that there would be living Seed upon the dying Earth. Life for the disciples after the coming of the Holy Spirit exploded into LIFE. A handful of believers multiplied into millions. The Spirit flowed from them. They loved the unlovable, defeated Satan as He tested them. They were love slaves of the living God. They faced conflict with truth. They were betrayed. They were taken captive yet remained free. They were falsely accused, taken to prison. They lost their lives by the thousands. The martyrs were burned at the stake, crucified, eaten by lions. The Living Seed multiplied and multiplied as it was placed into the Earth.

Have you been surprised at the path of a Life-giver as he/she follows the great Life-giver?   The Life-giver experiences over and over again the miracle of resurrection. Our natural life has no capacity to bring forth Eternal Life. His Life does. "Whoever desires to come after Me, let him deny himself, and take up his cross, and follow Me. (Mk.8:34) This pathway is narrow; few find it. Those who do, "know the Lord, the power of the resurrection, and the fellowship of His suffering."

> I have been crucified with Christ; it is no longer I who live, but Christ lives in me; and the life which I now live in the flesh I live by faith in the Son of God, who loved